# FROGMAN STORIES

# FROGMAN STORIES

Life and Leadership Lessons from the SEAL Teams

RICK KAISER

CASEMATE

*Philadelphia & Oxford*

Published in the United States of America and Great Britain in 2023 by
CASEMATE PUBLISHERS
1950 Lawrence Road, Havertown, PA 19083, USA
and
The Old Music Hall, 106–108 Cowley Road, Oxford OX4 1JE, UK

Paperback Edition: ISBN 978-1-63624-351-1
Digital Edition: ISBN 978-1-63624-352-8

A CIP record for this book is available from the British Library

Printed and bound in the United Kingdom by CPI Group (UK) Ltd, Croydon, CR0 4YY
Typeset in India by DiTech Publishing Services

For a complete list of Casemate titles, please contact:

CASEMATE PUBLISHERS (US)
Telephone (610) 853-9131
Fax (610) 853-9146
Email: casemate@casematepublishers.com
www.casematepublishers.com

CASEMATE PUBLISHERS (UK)
Telephone (0)1226 734350
Email: casemate-uk@casematepublishers.co.uk
www.casematepublishers.co.uk

*Front cover image:* Navy Frogman attaching explosives to ship. (The National Navy SEAL Museum)

# Contents

# Acknowledgements

I have countless people to credit for my success and where I am today. Surrounding myself with like-minded people has helped me feed off their energy during good times and bad. The mission is everything, whether it be an actual combat mission or the mission of the National Navy SEAL Museum. Find that mission. Write it down if you must and use it to guide your path. Deviate when you have to but come back on course as soon as possible. Accept help and guidance from others, but ultimately you are the one in control of your destiny.

I can't tell you what I would have done all those years ago if I had either quit or been injured during SEAL training. Dwelling on anything you have no control over is a distraction from the mission. Laser focus is the key; it has served me well. As I look back at my life and career, I realize many of the things that happened to me, good or bad, were out of my control. I just set myself up to be in the best position possible no matter what happened. All in all, it worked out in my favor, from my initial boss Rudy Boesch to taking the helm of the Navy SEAL Museum.

Thank You.
To my wife Barbara for your love and support at all times.
To Emily and Eric for being the best kids any father could hope for.
To Helen and Jim for teaching me what is important in life.
To Hector and Michelle for teaching me to have fun no matter what.
To the Navy SEAL Museum Team in Florida and California and the crew at NSWDG for all your selfless hard work in support of others.

# The U.S. Navy SEAL Ethos

In times of war or uncertainty there is a special breed of warrior ready to answer our Nation's call. A common man with uncommon desire to succeed. Forged by adversity, he stands alongside America's finest special operations forces to serve his country, the American people, and protect their way of life. I am that man.

My Trident is a symbol of honor and heritage. Bestowed upon me by the heroes that have gone before, it embodies the trust of those I have sworn to protect. By wearing the Trident, I accept the responsibility of my chosen profession and way of life. It is a privilege that I must earn every day.

My loyalty to Country and Team is beyond reproach. I humbly serve as a guardian to my fellow Americans always ready to defend those who are unable to defend themselves. I do not advertise the nature of my work, nor seek recognition for my actions. I voluntarily accept the inherent hazards of my profession, placing the welfare and security of others before my own.

I serve with honor on and off the battlefield. The ability to control my emotions and my actions, regardless of circumstance, sets me apart from other men. Uncompromising integrity is my standard. My character and honor are steadfast. My word is my bond.

We expect to lead and be led. In the absence of orders, I will take charge, lead my teammates and accomplish the mission. I lead by example in all situations.

I will never quit. I persevere and thrive on adversity. My Nation expects me to be physically harder and mentally stronger than my enemies. If knocked down, I will get back up, every time. I will draw on every remaining ounce of strength to protect my teammates and to accomplish our mission. I am never out of the fight.

We demand discipline. We expect innovation. The lives of my teammates and the success of our mission depend on me—my technical skill, tactical proficiency, and attention to detail. My training is never complete.

We train for war and fight to win. I stand ready to bring the full spectrum of combat power to bear in order to achieve my mission and the goals established by my country. The execution of my duties will be swift and violent when required yet guided by the very principles that I serve to defend.

Brave men have fought and died building the proud tradition and feared reputation that I am bound to uphold. In the worst of conditions, the legacy of my teammates steadies my resolve and silently guides my every deed. I will not fail.

CHAPTER I

# Prologue

Not all leaders are born. As in my case, years of being raised correctly and then a lifetime in the U.S. Navy have honed my abilities and taught me how to lead. No one can go to where they want to be without conflict along the way. Whether it be personal relationships or actual fighting on the battlefield, everyone has scars which hopefully remind us of how we got here in the first place. It is how you use those scars that make you an effective leader. Leading is not a popularity contest. If you hope to make friends and influence others, forget it. You may as well stay in bed, no need to make it. No one who makes the hard calls is loved by all. That is a falsity from other books and war movies.

I have thought about writing this book for some time now. I am not sure why this is the time but, as in all things in life, if you don't try, nothing is going to change. I have been fortunate to be led by some of the greatest warriors on the planet. I have also been unfortunate to be led by some of the worst examples of incompetence known to man. Gratefully, I have had far more great leaders than not. My only advice is to hang on and survive during the bad times. If you are expecting a tell-all book about Navy SEALs, forget it. Give the book away to someone else. This is simply my attempt to portray the Teams like they really are through humor and a few choice tidbits of knowledge earned the hard way. I'm sure not all will see the humor in my stories, but that is okay. Like I am known to say around the workplace, they can kiss my ass. Get a sense of humor and stop taking yourself so seriously. Put down the phone. Sign off of Myspace (joke) and do something productive.

I was born and raised in a small town named Oak Creek, Wisconsin, on the south side of Milwaukee. My parents, Elmer and Laverne Kaiser, raised me along with two brothers and two sisters in a small three-bedroom, one-bath home. I didn't think about it that much at the time, but it is amazing how seven people lived and got along with one bathroom. My mother was a saint. She managed to run our household, lead five children and a husband, on the very modest salary my father earned as a local firefighter. She is the one who taught me from the start that you don't have to be the loudest person in the room to accomplish your goals. Subtlety is an art learned over time. Picking your battles is another. Not all issues are worth falling on your sword. I have witnessed many leaders create chaos over every issue only to have the truly important problems glossed over or ignored altogether. My mother was soft spoken but got her point across through love and understanding. Letting her down was one of my greatest fears growing up, not because I would receive a beating—just the thought of disappointing her would crush my soul. A person who is that good is loved and respected by all who know them. I know I could never be that person, nor do I want to be. However, her teachings throughout my life have served me well. In fact, every time I have lost my temper or acted out of anger, I have regretted my actions because, in the end, I lost credibility and made poor choices. Taking a deep breath, waiting 24 hours, and talking to others will always serve you better than yelling or brute force. Remember, I said "try" to do the right thing.

Unfortunately, while growing up I suffered from BSU disease—Big, Slow and Uncoordinated. Fortunately, this ended up helping me immensely in the long run. I tried to be a jock but never quite had the skills to succeed at a high level in any sports. My brothers had better luck, but it was my two sisters who were the real athletes in my family (sorry, Mike and Bob) and well known in the state of Wisconsin on the volleyball and basketball courts. Me on the other hand, not so much. I tried out for the basketball team in my freshman year of high school because it was what all my friends were doing. When I look back on it now, I think I was cut after exiting the locker room on the way to the court. Never one to quit, I decided to try out for the swim team.

At that time, I knew how to doggie paddle and not drown; that was about it. Why I wanted to join the swim team is still a mystery to me. The coach decided to give me a chance and put me in the diving well away from the team, so I could learn how to swim properly with some guidance. I know that sort of thing doesn't happen anymore when trying out for high school sports, but it worked out for me. Not only was I winning races by the time I was a senior, but the swimming skills and confidence I learned in the water have served me well from Basic Underwater Demolition SEAL training to the present. Never quit.

I had always had a fascination with the ocean as a kid due to the show *The Undersea World of Jacques Cousteau*. I liked the water and swimming, which my high school swimming career had solidified in my mind. At the time I believed the U.S. Navy's submarine service was the right choice for me. That changed after my first trip to the Navy recruiter's office in South Milwaukee, Wisconsin. Lo and behold on his desk was a marketing pamphlet for Navy SEALs titled "The men with green faces." I picked it up and started looking at the pictures. I thought to myself, "This is badass, this is what I want to do." SEAL = SEA, AIR, LAND. Dive, jump, shoot, my dream come true. I was clueless. I asked the recruiter if I could take the pamphlet home. He didn't care because if it got him another number for his quota, he was all for it. He didn't know what a SEAL was either.

After contemplating the pamphlet for 48 hours, I decided I was going to pull the trigger and sign up to be a Navy SEAL. The recruiter was happy until he realized I had to pass the Navy's initial entrance exam at a higher level than the average sailor, and there was a physical screening test involved. I was a good student and didn't have any problem with the written test. The physical testing would be a bit different. I knew I could pass the standard. I made an appointment with my mother (I was 17 at the time) to visit Great Lakes Recruit Training Command and take the test with a real Navy SEAL running it. We drove down to Chicago on a Friday evening in the middle of winter in the Midwest. It was cold and snowing. The first portion of the test was inside at the pool along with the pull-ups, push-ups, and sit-ups. The run, however, was outside on the track next to the pool. A little whining here; the track was covered with snow, the temperature was easily below zero with wind chill, and I was wet with sweat and pool water. My first Navy SEAL test. I made the run under time and passed the physical screening test. The SEAL never came outside. That should have told me something.

The fact I was 17 at the time and I wanted to join the Navy caused a bit of an uproar at the Kaiser household. Because I was 17, it meant one of my parents had to sign the paperwork for me to enlist. Neither Mom nor Dad was in a big hurry to sign the papers. I guess they had fresh memories of Vietnam on their minds that I wasn't tracking at all. What high school kid was? Eventually, one of them signed the paperwork. I am grateful to them both for the trust they put in me.

# CHAPTER 2

# Hold the Standard

I graduated Basic Underwater Demolition SEAL Training (BUD/S) at the age of 18 as part of Class 109 in the summer of 1980. Soon thereafter, I reported for duty at SEAL Team TWO (ST-2) in Little Creek, Virginia. Command Master Chief (CMC) Rudy Boesch was the senior enlisted man on board and trusted advisor to the Commanding Officer. Rudy was in charge of managing a team of nearly one hundred Navy SEALs and other support personnel. He had already been in the U.S. Navy for over thirty years when I arrived at ST-2. In fact, Rudy had been a Master Chief—the highest enlisted rank in the Navy—for longer than I had been alive.

When the Japanese attacked Pearl Harbor on December 7, 1941, Navy Frogmen did not exist. The term "Frogman" refers to all units past and present of Naval Special Warfare—Naval Combat Demolition Units (NCDU); Underwater Demolition Teams (UDT); Scouts and Raiders (S&R); OSS Maritime Swimmers (Office of Strategic Services, precursor to the CIA); and present-day U.S. Navy SEAL Teams—but did not come into being until the Korean War. I am sure all our predecessors are proud to use the name. The Navy needed tough men skilled in all types of warfare to carry out some of the most difficult and dangerous missions of World War II. Their primary mission: reconnoiter enemy held beaches and destroy obstacles, man-made and natural, that would slow down landing craft during amphibious landings. In 1942, there were no tactics, techniques, or procedures to accomplish this mission. The Frogmen had to develop the skills necessary on their own with the limited experience of a few leaders such as Lt. Draper Kauffman, who was, at the time, one of the few explosives experts in the Navy. Explosives are the tool of choice for all Navy SEALs. One of my many mottos growing up through the Teams was "When in doubt, overload"; if you're not sure whether the explosives you've brought will do the job, add more.

One of the men who volunteered for this hazardous duty and completed S&R training during World War II was Rudy Boesch. Imagine joining the Navy during the war, volunteering for S&R training, getting on a train in Norfolk, Virginia, and traveling to Fort Pierce, Florida (the birthplace of Naval Special Warfare), only to immediately start "Hell Week" upon arrival. There was no time for hand holding. They had to be trained to fight both the Germans and the Japanese as fast as possible. Within 12 months, the original Frogmen had to adapt to, and overcome, a type of warfare that had not existed before that time. Scouts and Raiders were assigned missions similar to what Navy SEALs do today. Attack from the sea, recon enemy held territory, and take-out critical infrastructure such as bridges and railroad tracks. Unconventional warfare.

As with all wars, the United States has a tendency to downsize immediately following the conflict. World War II was no exception and the entire unit of Scouts and Raiders was disbanded. Rudy then volunteered for the famed UDTs who fought in the Pacific on what was an island-hopping strategy on the way to Japan. Rudy remained a UDT member through the Korean War and many other unnamed or unacknowledged conflicts until 1962 when President John F. Kennedy signed the official paperwork which created the first two SEAL Teams—SEAL Team ONE based in Coronado, California, and SEAL Team TWO based in Little Creek, Virginia. Rudy was a plank owner (original member) of the legendary Team TWO. The SEAL Teams—or Sea, Air, Land Teams—were created to fight in the deltas and rivers of Vietnam. As with his forefathers of the NCDUs, UDTs, and S&R, there was no playbook for the Navy SEALs. They had to create it and they were successful. Like their predecessors from World War II, many of the tactics and techniques the original SEALs created were still being used in the caves of Afghanistan to the deserts of Iraq.

Junior enlisted men such as I don't spend a lot of time with the CMC unless there is a specific reason (usually discipline). Luckily, I kept my nose relatively clean and avoided Rudy's gaze. When I had the chance to finally meet the man, I was understandably nervous. Here was a World War II, Korea, and Vietnam SEAL who had been there and done that for decades. What could he possibly want with me? I walked into his office, stood at attention, and waited for the secrets of being a SEAL. What he said instead was, "Kaiser, keep your uniform squared away and your hair cut. Come see me in six months and I will decide if you get your Trident or not."

What? Does he not understand I just completed SEAL training? Shouldn't he be telling me war stories? How can I be a badass SEAL like he is? Well, that is all I got but, honestly, it was some of the best guidance I ever received in the Teams. What I didn't understand at the time was what that one sentence actually meant—maintain the standard or face the consequences.

SEALs have a way of pushing or testing the rules which is hammered into your soul starting with BUD/S training. The instructors want two things from every candidate: quit in training, not in combat; and figure out a way to do every mission. Never quit. Rules about haircuts and uniforms mean little when you believe you can accomplish anything, no matter what the task. What Rudy did with that early guidance was lay down the law and set a standard. Do these two simple tasks and you will prove you are responsible for more. There is no gray area when it comes to a squared-away uniform or haircut. No room for interpretation; yes/no, black/white in a world that is anything but. Hold the standard.

When I received this brief guidance from Rudy, I said, "Yes, Master Chief" and left the office. Although a bit disappointed I had not learned how to take out a sentry with a ballpoint pen, at least I wasn't in trouble. SEALs have a tendency to get into trouble at times. It's in our DNA. The trick was to keep it to a minimum and never do anything to dishonor the Team. The absolute task that no SEAL or any person on this planet would enjoy is a duty called "standing quarterdeck watch." In a SEAL Team that means answering the phone and greeting people at the front door in proper uniform and with a good haircut. If you were lucky at ST-2, you would only have to stand duty for 24 hours every few weeks. Not too bad in the big picture, but I was a Navy SEAL. I didn't have time for that. My goals at that time were to go out on the town as often as I could and have as much fun as I could handle, like all 18-year-olds. What I didn't realize when he was laying down the order was how swift and effective the consequences and/or punishments were. All it took was one glance from Rudy with a follow-up statement: "SEAL X, go get a haircut and report to the quarterdeck." Nobody ever questioned or complained about the order. We knew when we were wrong and accepting the punishment was part of the price. If you were a habitual offender, Rudy would think of other duties even more painful to help you find your way: raking the leaves from the entire ST-2 compound; cleaning all the heads (bathrooms) in the building; or, worst of all, confinement to the Team for an extended period. Rudy's order served me well over my career. I made it a point to always have a good haircut and squared-away uniform. Two simple things I didn't have to worry about.

I remember a time in Bosnia in the late 1990s—when our mission was to hunt "persons indicted for war crimes"—when having long hair was approved for our Team in order to fit in with the local population. I thought it was going to be cool to have long hair, but I did not last three weeks before I was at the barber asking for a trim. I thought of myself as a Bosnian businessman rather than the Bosnian biker thugs all my teammates looked like.

I picked "Hold the Standard" as a theme in this book and my leadership style because it will work for any age from millennial to boomer. Everyone has probably heard this before in a different manner. It is always easier to loosen up than tighten up when it comes to discipline. "Hold the Standard" is the starting point.

Rudy always led from the front. He was always there taking part in every physical fitness event the Team had going each morning; whether it be an ocean swim in freezing water or multiple obstacle courses followed by a long run, Rudy was there. Never first, but also never last. As a young guy, I was impressed and hoped to be able to do the same thing as I got older.

CHAPTER 3

# There Are Two Ways to Do Things—the Right Way and Again

Basic Underwater Demolition SEAL (BUD/S) training is the initial six-month training pipeline that defines being a Navy SEAL. The easiest way to spot a fake SEAL is to ask what his BUD/S class number was. If he doesn't automatically come out with a number that makes sense, or says it is classified, he is a fraud.

When I went to BUD/S, I did not understand any of the history or heritage of Naval Special Warfare (NSW). Sad but true, NSW does a very poor job educating young Frogmen about the past. Many of the traditions carried out over eighty years ago at Fort Pierce are still done today. A typical BUD/S class to this day can be seen carrying rubber boats called IBS, or "Inflatable Boat Small" in Navy speak. For years, I believed it was just the BUD/S instructors' way of torturing prospective SEALs. Little did I know the Frogmen of World War II that infiltrated the beaches of Normandy paddled in these rubber boats full of explosives so they could destroy the German obstacles which lined the beaches. The boats were part of their life and critical to their mission.

Other traditions started in Fort Pierce such as the training of officers and enlisted men, log PT, and Hell Week. Log PT is simply that, physical training using a large log. Usually, a group of seven men would have to lift the log and work as a Team in order to move the log in whatever manner the instructor wanted. Hell Week was also started at Fort Pierce and was used as a way to test the men to perform their duties with little sleep while under constant pressure. I think it would have been helpful to know the reasons why we were doing certain activities; it would have given us a tie or bond to the Frogmen of the past. History and heritage must never be forgotten; they help us remember our beginnings and realize we are not special. Many men have fought and died through the years with a lot less recognition, training, and equipment than any of the current SEALs will ever know.

Every SEAL thinks their BUD/S class was the hardest ever. Every SEAL thinks they are the best SEAL (or at least they should). If not, you may as well go home because you don't belong. Seems rough, but without that way of thinking it will be impossible to lead. I didn't believe I was the best SEAL while going through BUD/S training. I was a fair athlete. I could run, I could swim, and I was fairly mentally tough. My two sisters were the real athletes in my family. My two brothers and I had to take a back seat to their accomplishments. I fully acknowledge their achievements, but it still tends to become a joke when we get together and talk about high school, especially after I completed BUD/S.

BUD/S training for the most part is a mental and physical grind. If you can survive the day-to-day routine of pain and cold, you can complete BUD/S. My weakness was, and always will be, push-ups (long arms not built for explosive strength, more a distance athlete). Of course, push-ups were a daily torture I dreaded at BUD/S. Never-ending push-ups were always on my mind. It was easy for the instructors to see who was struggling and who wasn't. I was punished immensely through BUD/S for my lack of push-up skill. The pain even started before BUD/S officially did. Class 109 was to start on a Monday. Part of the tradition of BUD/S is for the prospective class of over 150 guys to shave their heads to prepare for the first day of training. Hair only gets in the way during training. As we were drinking and celebrating our new lives, a few individuals thought it would be a good idea to grab a random sailor from the beach where we were shaving heads and also shave his head. Bad idea. The poor guy never had a chance. No one listened to his screams of terror. Many didn't even know he wasn't even going through BUD/S. The incident lasted no longer than five minutes and the sailor was gone, never to be seen again, or so we thought. The next morning, we all got in formation and waited for our instructors to begin. As we stood in front of the barracks for over an hour, we started to wonder what was going on. Our answers came very quickly in the form of the Commanding Officer (CO) of BUD/S training. He proceeded to drop us in the push-up position and begin a lecture on why we had made a tremendous mistake shaving the head of a random sailor the day before. As it turns out, the sailor was a junior officer going to fleet training at Coronado Amphibious Base. He was not happy, his Commanding Officer was not happy, and our CO was pissed.

We stayed in the push-up position for over an hour until our noodle arms could take no more. Then we all lined up so the shaved officer could walk by each and every one of us so he could identify the culprits that shaved his head. To this day, I am not sure if the officer really didn't recognize the guys that shaved his head or if he had made a deal with the CO to scare us. Either way, he walked by each of us and left. We had sufficient rest at that point to be dropped once again for another hour until training officially began. This was going to be hell. I hate push-ups.

A typical BUD/S class has around a seventy percent or higher attrition rate. Class 109 was no different. We started with approximately 150 men and finished with 30. What I finally figured out after living through the first month of BUD/S training was, just like the getting a haircut analogy, the instructors had black and white rules to guide their actions. Number one, they can't kill you. Sure, they could make you suffer, but not to the point of physical harm. Number two, no matter how bad it gets, they can't take your birthday away and your mother will love you regardless of the outcome of SEAL training. Number three, they will not let you out of the cold water until the medical guidelines of hypothermia are met. In other words, taking into account body weight and water temperature, a human can survive a specified amount of time in cold water; cut and dried, tried and true numbers monitored by medical professionals. The hypothermia guideline states if the water temperature is between 50–60 degrees, an individual can last 1–2 hours before exhaustion or unconsciousness. The first time my class of SEAL candidates was put in the 60-degree Pacific Ocean, we had no clue about hypothermia charts. All we knew was the water was cold and no one was going to quit. Thirty minutes later, the instructors offered the class a deal. If someone quit, we could all get out of the water. At that point, no one was shaking to the point of quitting. Thirty more minutes into the evolution, however, the first hand went up and the classmate was escorted from the water never to be seen again. Thinking we were all getting out any minute, the instructors made another deal. First, since the individual quit 30 minutes after the first deal, it was invalid. Second, if we wanted to get out of the water, it would now take two people quitting. The next two people inevitably quit but the stakes kept getting higher. By the time we actually got out of the water, the number was five candidates. They were not going to let us out until the medical chart said they had to. The key to BUD/S training—they can't kill you and no one is taking your birthday away. We never got out of the water early.

We lost most of our people in the first five weeks of training before and during Hell Week, which was designed to break you down to your absolute breaking point to test if you could still operate and complete the mission. In the case of Hell Week, the breakdown came from a lack of sleep for over five days and nights while constantly performing physical and mental training exercises. Anyone who tells you they did not consider quitting is probably lying. My time to consider quitting came on Wednesday night, day three of Hell Week.

Due to lack of sleep and constant activity, BUD/S students are fed four times a day to offset the drain of energy. On night three, at approximately 0100, what was left of the class sat down for a nice hot meal in an extremely warm and dry chow hall. Our only instruction was "Do not fall asleep!" Needless to say, we all fell asleep within minutes. We did not know the instructors had actually turned up the thermostat to help the process—not that we actually needed any help.

For what seemed like hours, but was actually minutes, we slept—fat, dumb and happy—until the instructors, in a choreographed move, burst through the doors and started yelling for everyone to wake up and move outside in formation. This was the time I felt most sorry for myself. I was warm and my stomach was full. What was I doing? Why was I putting myself through this torture? Unbeknown to the instructors, they actually helped save me that night. Part of their punishment for falling asleep was to put the class into the cold water of Coronado Bay to help us see the error in our ways. The shock of the cold water was the catalyst

I needed to wake up and stop the negative thinking that had taken over in the chow hall. It was at that point I knew I could make it the rest of the way through Hell Week.

As we stood in the water up to our chests, the instructors had us link arms. We were told that at the count of three, if everyone was to put their heads underwater for a count of three seconds, they would let the class out of the water. Simple, we can do that. The first attempt went without a hitch. We surfaced expecting to get out when one of the instructors informed us someone on the left flank did not get their head all the way under the water. He couldn't exactly see who it was because it was dark. We were pissed at whomever it was, but we could do it again and get out. The next attempt produced the same results but this time on the right flank. The instructors again couldn't quite make out who did not stick their head totally under the water. This process went on for at least another five to six attempts until we finally realized the instructors were playing a psychological game with us. We had been playing the game correctly; they were never going to let us out.

BUD/S instructors are masters of pain. They know just how to make you quit and that is exactly what they all want. They want the quitters to leave during training and not during combat. Makes sense but not while you are suffering through it. Once the class became "enlightened to the torture," the dunking of the heads became sloppy and no one really tried any more so the instructors came up with another test. If any man could get an erection, the instructors would let us all out of the cold water. No way, too cold, too tired. That is until my partner next to me delinked his arms and began to rub his nipple with one hand and penis with the other. He closed his eyes and leaned his head back as we all stood and watched. To our amazement, he actually got an erection. Everyone was impressed, including the instructors. They let us out of the water and led us on to our next evolution. Even BUD/S instructors have a sense of right and wrong. It doesn't happen that often, but some things are impressive.

The rest of Hell Week was a blur. My remaining teammates and I were just trying to survive at this point. Quitting was not an option. The only thing that was always looming in the back of your mind was an injury that would force you to quit. Getting hurt any time during Hell Week meant you would have to start over from day one should you want to give it another try.

The best way to stay on track during BUD/S is to do exactly what the instructors ask or give it your very best attempt. The guys that looked for short cuts or pushed their work off on their teammates were usually the first ones to quit. Something as easy as keeping your barracks room clean could turn into a nightmare on any morning. Part of the instructors' duty was to do an inspection each day to ensure the students were taking care of their rooms and equipment. It was easy to see the guys that didn't pay attention to detail; they ended up being the favorites of the instructors each morning. You either clean your room the right way each day or you end up doing it again after you are forced to "hit the surf," roll around in the sand, and return to your room. The pain could always be avoided if you had just done it right the first time. I did not mind watching others go through the torture, because that meant my roommates and I were being left alone. We even left things like fruit and other snacks in our room so the instructors inspecting the room could have a treat on their way to mess with my friends in the next room. Of course, it didn't always work out in our favor, but we tried to make our trips to the surf zone as few as possible.

# CHAPTER 4

# Worn but Not Worn Out

At the time I graduated Basic Underwater Demolition SEAL (BUD/S) training in the fall of 1980, both SEAL Teams and Underwater Demolition Teams (UDT) existed in the U.S. Navy. The "Needs of the Navy" always come first, but they do ask you what your preference of duty station would be. In my case, it was SEAL Team TWO (ST-2), UDT 21, and UDT 22 in that order. All East Coast Teams were based out of Little Creek, Virginia. There were two major reasons for this request which I could never have realized the future implications of: Virginia was much closer to my home state of Wisconsin, which would make it easier and faster for visits; and the drinking age at the time in Virginia was 18 while California was 21. I didn't think it was fair to have to wait three years to be able to have a legal drink while at the same time risking your neck as a Navy SEAL. To this day, I think this country has some soul searching to do regarding this subject. How can an 18-year-old be responsible enough to join the military and risk their life, and also vote for the President of the United States, but not be able to have a drink at the bar or buy a pack of cigarettes? It should be one age or the other for all, or at least give military members under 21 a waiver while on active duty.

I got lucky and received orders to ST-2. My timing was perfect for assignment to ST-2 because ST-6 was just forming up and many of the new members of ST-6 came directly from ST-2, leaving a vacancy for new guys like me. I often think what it would have been like to have gone to a UDT instead of ST-2. Would I have stayed in the Navy? Who knows, no time to dwell on hypotheticals.

When SEALs aren't fighting, they are training. Most of our lives were actually spent on a training schedule to prepare for war. The first such training after BUD/S was called SEAL Basic Training (SBT). When I first got to ST-2 out of BUD/S, I was on a short pause while waiting on my SBT class to form up. Also, since I had just arrived at the Team, I was low man on the totem pole ready for any shitty little job that would come up. I didn't mind the work, but I did mind being placed in a barracks with three roommates I didn't know. I had just lived through six months of arguably the toughest military training on the planet and time to get away to your own space was critical. I didn't have long to worry about it, however, because I was assigned to Master Chief Boesch as his assistant at Fort A. P. Hill running the current SBT class. No rest for the weary, but at least I wasn't stuck on base. Fortunately for me, this was a good time when I got to know Rudy and I was lucky to learn from him as he assisted the other instructors training the new SEALs. I lived in a converted Conex (container, express) box for the next two months; tough living with mediocre food, much of which I prepared daily with Rudy. At the time, I could never quite figure out why the Master Chief was the guy running the chow hall and not the training. It seemed like a waste of talent to me. What I came to find out was Rudy had been the Command Master Chief at ST-2 for such a long time that he wanted to give the other instructors, many of whom were Vietnam veterans, the chance to run the show without him looking over their shoulders. Even at his rank and experience, he was always willing to take the shit job to best complete the mission.

I lived there for the next two months until it was time for my SBT class to form up. By the time I got back to Little Creek, I had received permission to move off base and get my first apartment. Hooyah. As I was packing my clothing up in the barracks I had only slept in one night, I found a marijuana pipe and a bag of weed in my locker. Somehow my "roommates" had figured out a way to open my locker and stash their drugs in it so I would be the one to get busted should the drug dog come by. Needless to say, I was angry and looking for retribution but, luckily for all concerned, my roommates were not around. I threw the pot away and left the barracks for good. The reason I bring this up is because I often thought afterward what would have happened to me if the drugs had been discovered. How would my life have been changed? Everyone always claims the drugs are not theirs when they are caught. I dodged a major bullet on that one and it helped me realize not all people are guilty of crimes just because it appears that way.

When SBT started, I was as ready as I was ever going to be. What I wasn't ready for, however, was the actual equipment issued to us for the training. Most was worn out World War II/Korea-era gear. The Teams of the past were not like the Teams of today; they had no budget. Mother Navy looked at the SEAL Teams as an afterthought that took money from their beloved aircraft carriers, submarines, and jets. That was a hard realization coming to the Teams straight out of BUD/S training; we were not actually the center of the universe. Lack of equipment and food meant we had to buy our own. I remember to this day that I earned $411 a month at that time and was happy to get it. Food and berthing money were supplied, so I had plenty to save up to buy boots, a sleeping bag, gloves, a wool hat, sunglasses, a backpack, and other necessary equipment. This may be the reason why most SEALs did not look uniform in appearance while operating. We didn't have a choice. Food was no different. We were given C-rations, originally issued in World War II, which included such delicacies as pressed meat and cigarettes. Yum. I never really thought about it that much until I was older. I thought Navy SEALs were the best of the best. Who would have known the U.S. Navy didn't feel the same way at the time? When I made it to ST-2, SEALs were organized into 16-man platoons modeled after our structure in Vietnam. Two officers, one chief, one leading petty officer, and 12 knuckle draggers. We were a very tight group. We did not get along all the time but, for the most part, we knew what we had to do to get the job done. Our job was to keep each other alive and complete any mission, training or real world, handed to us. Buying our own equipment and food was part of the deal. Easy day.

# CHAPTER 5

# No Matter How Bad You Have It, It Can Always Be Worse

As a winter warrior in my SEAL Team TWO days, our mission during the Cold War was to be ready to support our NATO allies in Scandinavia in case of Russian invasion. Seems hard to believe now in the age of the Taliban and ISIS but that is what we did. I was lucky enough to learn from the best—the Norwegian Jaegers. They were master cross-country skiers and could survive in the frozen mountains of Norway for extended periods of time. Winter warfare is an art; not only must you be ready to face the enemy at any time, but you must also fight the environment, which can prove to be even more deadly. Training and clothing are critical to survival. No one is coming to save you should you run into trouble; you must rely on your teammates, equipment, and experience to survive such harsh conditions.

Frostbite was always a factor. Best case, you would lose the feeling in your feet or hands for an extended period of time. Worst case, you would lose some fingers, or toes, or worse. Attention to detail was paramount along with knowing your equipment. Body heat and sweat were also factors to worry about. Any water on your body in the winter can drive your body temperature down to hypothermic ranges very quickly. It was a fine dance between staying comfortable while moving with a ton of equipment and overheating and sweating no matter how cold it was outside. Typical areas that needed the most protection were hands and feet. Less blood flow means less body heat. We typically patrolled with a light pair of camouflage pants and possibly an over-white covering to blend in with the snow. On top was usually the same lightweight covering which allowed all the heat you were producing to escape and not cause perspiration. If you had to stop for longer than five minutes for any reason, each of us had a warm jacket to put on to trap the heat before we started moving again. Winter warfare is definitely a thinking man's game. No time to relax, you are always threatened by something.

One of the more important skills we were taught was called "camp routine." After finding a suitable place to set up camp, personnel were assigned to create deception trails, set up booby traps, and start a security watch. The snow tends to give away your position should someone be looking for you. Once all that was completed, everyone was cleared to set up their two-man tents as fast as humanly possible. We were experts at setting up our tent. Wasted minutes fumbling around meant lost body heat which led to frostbite and hypothermia or, worse yet, failing your mission. I remember many a night laughing at some of my friends from inside the comfort of my sleeping bag while they struggled to erect their tent. No mercy for the unprepared. To this day, I remember the procedures and order my tent buddy and I used to set up camp:

1. With your skis on, tramp down an area the same size as the tent.
2. Remove skis and place tail ends in the snow, poles tied on top. This is done to keep snow and ice off the working surface (bottom).
3. Place vapor barrier (space blanket) on the snow foil side down and place tent on top of it. Place three poles in tent, tie or stake as necessary.
4. Place weapon, backpack, and other equipment inside tent vestibule at both ends of tent.
5. Lay out ground pad, sleeping bag, stove, and candle for light inside tent.
6. Remove boots and remove any snow on them. Do not bring snow into the tent.
7. Crawl in sleeping bag and light stove. There is some controversy here. Some would say never light the stove inside the tent. Others, not so much. We always used our stove inside the tent even though I did watch another team's tent go up in flames. Pays to be careful.

8. Melt snow for your drinking water, then for your meal.
9. Eat with the biggest spoon you can find in order to get more food than your partner.
10. Clean up, take a Motrin, and a shot of whiskey. Wipe your face and pits with a wet wipe and go to sleep. Place your boots inside your sleeping bag so they don't freeze. Remove as much clothing as possible and place on top of your body so it will dry overnight.

The only way to survive multiple days or weeks in the Arctic is to feed the machine. A constant supply of calories is necessary if you are going to ski all day up and down vast mountain ranges. Meal planning is essential to ensure you have enough food to last throughout the mission. Weight is also a critical factor in winter warfare; it adds up fairly quickly when talking about tents, stoves, fuel, food, sleeping bags, ski wax, spare parts, radios, and batteries, not to mention a full combat load of weapons and ammunition. A typical load was 100–120 lbs. There was a fine line between traveling lighter but freezing at night because you didn't have the proper gear. The weaker skiers had a tough time keeping up.

Back to the food. Most food in America and in the U.S. military comes over-packaged. Since weight and space were closely watched, we had to break down each meal by contents and repackage each. A typical dinner meal consisted of two dehydrated Long Range Patrol Rations, two ramen noodles, an entire stick of butter (for added calories), and enough spices and hot sauce to make it taste good. Water was abundant all around us so that was not a problem; it just had to be melted and added to the meals. Although the meal does not sound appetizing, it was one of the only things to look forward to at the end of the day.

I was fortunate enough to be one of the better skiers and was often assigned as point man unless I was taking a break further back in the patrol. I liked the job, but breaking trail all day in deep snow wasn't much fun. Once the snow is compacted into two ski tracks, everyone else can move as cross-country skis are intended to be used. Point usually involved stepping a foot or two up and then shifting downward with each stride. Not whining, just stating the facts. Route planning was critical. You can't go up or down at too steep an angle. Traversing was the key to success in either direction. Moving down a hill at a high rate of speed with a heavy pack is a recipe for disaster. Sudden stops from trees could break bones or kill you. One thing you had to keep your eye out for was small pine trees in your path. The trees were not actually small at all but the very top of a large tree buried underneath the snow. It was easy to ski too close to one of these trees and fall headfirst up to 15–20 feet. I watched one of my teammates do that very same thing and it took him 20 minutes to work himself out of the hole while the rest of the Team stood around and laughed. There really wasn't much we could do to assist for fear of falling in ourselves and making the matter worse. By the time he got out he was soaking wet and yelling "F— God"! When we started moving again, not 10 minutes had passed before the whole thing happened again to the same guy. What a glorious day; I still laugh when I think about it.

One thing no one thinks or talks about in winter warfare is going to the bathroom. Number 1 is easy. Find a tree so you don't leave a big yellow mark in the snow. Number 2 is a bit tricky. When it is 10 degrees below zero, and you're packed snug and sound inside your sleeping bag at 0200, the last thing you want to do is go outside. Constipation is a real threat. Bottom line: don't hold it. Eating 4–5,000 calories a day creates a lot of back up. No matter how cold it is you have to go. One of my favorite things to do during these wonderful moments was to sneak over to another team's vestibule, slowly open the zipper, do my business, and sneak back to my tent. Listening to angry Frogmen first thing in the morning is quite hilarious. Don't worry, the gift was frozen by morning and, without DNA testing, there was no way to find out exactly who was doing the dirty work unless you got caught in the act. Funny what your mind comes up with. Small things make me happy.

Breaking camp was even more important than setting up, typically 30 minutes before the sun came up, but an exact time was given to the Team to be ready to move. No gray area, not a minute before or after. Everyone was depending on each other to be ready to go. Movement meant warmth. Standing still meant frostbite and cold injuries, not to mention some very angry teammates who tended to beat the latecomers post-mission. Getting a haircut at that point seemed trivial to losing a finger or toe because someone couldn't follow orders. Even with the best-trained team, I can remember times when I lost the feeling in my toes for months just trying to operate in the winter wonderland. Set your left and right boundaries, no compromise. People do not live up to low expectations. Set the standard and they will comply. Retrain the ones having trouble and cut away the ones that are untrainable, or at least move them on to a less demanding job. In a SEAL Team, that means out of your platoon and into an administrative role. Yes, SEALs are no different than anyone else. The good, the bad, and the ugly. We just happen to be better trained than most. You learn very quickly who you can depend on to get the job done and who you cannot.

No one is perfect, including the Master Chief. Another of my favorite places for winter-warfare training was Goose Bay, Labrador, in northeast Canada. The base was jointly run by the Canadian and American militaries. I have never seen so much snow or been so cold in my life and that is saying a lot for someone born and raised in Wisconsin. It was also the perfect place to hone your winter-warfare skills. No distractions, just snow, cold, and great expanses of land. While conducting winter-warfare training in Goose Bay, we were dropped off by helicopter at a random peak in the Newfoundland countryside in order to navigate our way off the mountain and meet Rudy at a pre-planned resupply point miles away. All went as planned. The Huey touched down on the top of a snow-covered mountain. We exited the helicopter and proceeded to figure out where we were. No GPS back then, just good old map and compass. Once we figured out our location, the next step was to plan a route that would lead us safely to the resupply point. Marching down the side of a mountain with a 100-lb backpack and combat load is no easy task, but that is what we were trained to do.

Not everything went as planned, however. On the trek down the mountain, there were a number of fast-moving streams and rivers we had to cross; beautiful clear and clean water between 34 to 40 degrees. During one of these crossings, one of my teammates slipped and fell into the rushing water and disappeared from our view. Everyone on the Team immediately dropped their backpack and moved downstream to recover whatever resurfaced. Luckily, our teammate and most of his equipment resurfaced about 100 yards down the river. We quickly pulled him out and got him inside his sleeping bag because he was already suffering from hypothermia. Cold water kills quickly; wet clothing kills just as quick. We started a fire to dry his clothes and equipment and noticed he was missing his weapon. In this case it was an M4. Shit. No one wants to report a missing weapon to their Commanding Officer. That sort of thing gets you shit-canned from the Teams. We couldn't blame the guy who lost it, because he was only trying to save his life. We spread out and searched for the weapon along the banks of the river. The water was flowing fast enough to carry the weapon anywhere. It seemed pretty hopeless. Our officer in charge (OIC) had the idea to throw another weapon, in this case an 870 Remington shotgun, in the water at the same point where the guy fell in to watch where it went. Of course, we were going to tie a climbing rope to the weapon so we wouldn't end up losing two weapons. In retrospect, probably not a great idea. We should have cut our losses and moved on. We tied the rope to the shotgun and threw it into the rushing river only for it to move about 10 yards and get stuck between two large boulders. Now what? No one could pull it out; it was stuck. The OIC looked around and asked for volunteers to go in and get it. We figured each man had about two minutes in the rushing water before they became useless and needed to be pulled out. Ever the Boy Scout, I was the first man in. I made it to the shotgun and actually put my hand on the weapon before I couldn't feel my fingers anymore. I used all my strength but no joy. I gave it one more try before my teammates pulled me out and put me in my sleeping bag because I was shaking uncontrollably. I didn't see the second guy make the attempt because I was shaking so bad, but he ended up in the same condition. Our OIC finally made the decision to give up the effort, accept the loss, and move on to whatever awaited him when we got back to the team. Turns out he was not shit-canned from the team, which we all were grateful for, but the ridicule from our teammates was relentless. We had no clever comebacks or excuses. We were all responsible and we all owned the mistake. No one died, we lost two weapons, and bore the brunt of jokes for quite a while. No matter how bad you have it, it can always be worse.

As we continued on our mission, after five days of constant movement, little rest, and limited rations, we were on time to meet Rudy at a predetermined rendezvous point. I was amazed the Master Chief had traveled all this way to support our training. He had already been in the Navy over thirty years but had never forgotten who he was and what was important to the guys. As we approached the rally point, we found Rudy, another teammate, and two cases of Old Milwaukee beer in an inflatable boat on the side of the lake where we were to meet. Both were sound asleep, no beer left, and no resupply of food or water. When we were able to wake him, he gave us a thumbs up for making it so far on schedule. He apologized for forgetting the food and water, asked for help putting the boat back in the water, and left us standing there with another 20 miles to go before ending the exercise. SEAL training at its finest. We knew he didn't forget the resupply; there never was a resupply. No matter how bad you have it, it can always be worse. Words to live by.

CHAPTER 6

# Keep Moving Forward

Psychological warfare is an everyday occurrence in the life of a SEAL. Testing limits, stamina, tolerance, and temper regularly keeps you ready for just about any situation. Losing the non-existent resupply was normal. Never quit, move on, and learn from the experience.

Mental toughness is something you are born with. Everyone has it, some are just better at using it than others. Inner strength knows no race, sex, social position, or age. I have found the more you use it, the stronger you become to withstand any type of adversity. Parents, teachers, and mentors who coddle you are not helping you in the long run. Sure, it is easier but, when the shit hits the fan, most are not prepared. There is no typical Navy SEAL. The Navy has spent millions of dollars trying to figure out what makes a SEAL and how they can recruit and produce more. Waste of money. There is no way to measure the mental toughness required to complete BUD/S training. The guys who are the most muscular, or possibly the best athletes, would be expected to excel at SEAL training. Not true. Working out, physical fitness, and sports all require a routine. A regular schedule and diet help to keep you in the best shape possible. What makes SEALs different is there is no schedule or consistent diet for any length of time. It is the guy who can overcome eating things such as "Meals Ready to Eat" three times a day for weeks on end and still perform at an advanced level. There is no way to measure the ability to perform after being locked up in a hotel room or sniper hide for a week. The point is, take what is given and learn to work with whatever is dealt. When you have free time, go work out. Doesn't matter what you do. Stay active.

During an exercise in northern Norway to monitor warship movements and report to higher headquarters, two SEALs and two Jaegers were given the task of skiing over 20 miles to get into position and then survive for a week while conducting the operation. Movement in the mountains to get into position without being detected is slow and arduous. Once we arrived, we quickly set up camp and began to observe the fjord below for movement. If it hadn't been so cold, I could have dealt with the boredom. I was content sitting inside my sleeping bag, observing and reporting, both of which are sloppy and lazy. My Norwegian counterpart insisted we go on twice daily patrols in order to secure the area. Not a great idea when you are trying to hide. After the third day, however, I realized it wasn't a patrol, but a reason to get up and out of our comfort zone, staying on edge mentally and physically no matter how much you didn't want to go out in the cold. It was the best standard operating procedure for the winter warrior I can remember. Being warm and dry with a full stomach does not help you complete your mission. In fact, discomfort is what keeps you laser focused on what you are doing. I'm not saying to deliberately make yourself miserable but, if everything is given to you, how will you react when things go sideways?

Case in point, as part of the same exercise that had us locked down on a mountainside observing ship movements, we were also tasked to harass and disrupt a much larger force of regular U.S. Army and Norwegian troops at a tent camp in the area. As we snuck into the camp one evening, it was obvious no one was awake to detect our movement. The goal was to create as much chaos as possible in the shortest amount of time and get the hell out. Getting caught by the Army would not only be embarrassing, but they would no doubt tie us to a tree for a while and let us suffer in the cold. As we moved into position, each man had their skis, poles, rifle, and two tear gas grenades. On cue, each pulled their pins and tossed their grenades inside the tents of our lazy counterparts. Needless to say, reaction was swift. Guys were running out of their tents cursing and ready for blood. As we moved away from the camp while being pursued, my teammate lost one of his skis and moved in a hop/ski method until we were well away from the now wide-awake camp. We recovered the rest of our equipment and proceeded to move off the mountain. The problem was my teammate was not capable of skiing with a backpack on one ski. One of our Jaeger friends was willing to try. To this day, I am still amazed how he was able to carry all that weight down a mountain on one ski. If the snow had not been so deep, we probably could have walked out, but not that day. We made it off the mountain three hours later exhausted and grateful to be on our way back to base. Had it not been for our Norwegian friends, I would probably still be on that mountain today.

Winter warfare is mentally exhausting. Fighting the cold, staying one step ahead of the enemy, and keeping your sanity night after night was one of the harder tests of my SEAL career. One thing I learned during this time, and on almost every deployment, was to "Never make any life-changing decisions about your future while on deployment." It is easy to start feeling sorry for yourself when you are far from home missing your family and your life. There is nothing wrong with thinking about those things from time to time, but dwelling on them will crush your soul. My rule of thumb was to wait for 10 days after returning home before making any decisions of consequence. After being home for a few days, nothing, including an extended deployment, seems that bad. After 10 days, it is a thing of the past and you are forced to move on to the next issue. I have offered up that advice to many a military member and it has never backfired. Even if the decision remains the same as on deployment, at least you took the time to consider all sides of the problem. Remove emotion and keep moving forward.

CHAPTER 7

# Plan Your Dive, Dive Your Plan

Close your eyes and imagine yourself in the darkest closet you have ever been in—so dark, you can't see your fingers in front of your face. Now imagine a large speaker with base playing so loud that your whole body shakes. Well, that is what it is like underneath a ship during a night ship attack. SEALs are known for their skill in, on, and under the water. That is what makes us different from all other Special Forces besides being better than they are (humble too).

Diving operations are inherently dangerous due to many factors—operating at night, breathing 100-percent oxygen from a re-breather, cold water, and boat traffic to name a few. The worst of all is practicing and conducting ship attacks. SEALs by themselves cannot carry enough explosives to sink a ship of any size; our goal is to disable a major component such as the rudder so the ship cannot get underway. Small charges with magnets and underwater timers are the ticket for that problem. Usually, two two-man teams set out on a mission like this. One team could do the job but, as the saying goes, "Two is one, one is none." Double your chances at success. Both pairs plan their dive and figure out the best route to the target. Remember, this is all done at night. Once you enter the water, you can no longer see anything besides your compass, depth gauge, and watch. Communication between teammates is conducted through a series of pre-determined squeezes. One squeeze means "Okay." Two means "Stop," etc. Divers are attached to each other by a rope with Velcro attachments called a buddy line in case you get separated in the dark. The lead diver navigates and sets pace to the target. Your goal is to move under the water at a predetermined pace and distance in order to hit the ship in just the right spot. Mistakes cost time and energy. For example, if you hit the bow of an aircraft carrier and meant to hit the stern, tack on another hour diving from one end to the other. The other diver is basically hanging on to the lead diver and is supposed to be looking out for obstacles. Most times you end up hitting the obstruction with your head full speed because of the darkness.

Diving underwater at night is already very dark; once you go underneath a ship it becomes black. Even the luminescent dials on your instruments are barely visible. A compass becomes useless within close proximity to a metal ship. You have to know from experience which way to go or you could end up running out of oxygen underneath the ship. Most people think of a ship's hull as being one continuous piece of metal. In fact, the hull is many large pieces of plate welded together. With no compass, the diver's job is to feel for the welds of the hull in order to move in a straight line. If you hit the wrong weld, you will only move to the side of the ship and risk detection. Your job is to move aft to the rudders and propellers, which are your main targets. While you are moving to the target feeling the weld, your hand needs to be in front of you at all times to detect suction. Ships are equipped with large suction pipes called sea chests which suck water into the ship to cool equipment. The sea chests also suck up divers. If you are lucky enough to keep your mouthpiece in your mouth if sucked up, you will just die in place when your oxygen runs out. Unfortunately, your dive buddy won't be able to help either. Best move at that point is to cut the safety line and complete the mission, or go for help should it be a training mission. If all goes smoothly, you swim directly to the rudder or propeller, place your charge, set the timer, and swim like hell out of there. The key to becoming a good combat swimmer (another name for SEAL) is always maintaining your composure. Controlling your emotions, heart rate, and breathing serves you well, whether underwater or 30,000 feet above the earth getting ready to make a parachute drop. Most of that composure comes from realistic training. When we aren't fighting, we are training to fight. It is the only way to get better and build muscle memory. If you have already been through something once, or at least close to the experience, it is much easier to stay calm. If the experience happens to be brand new, that is when you rely on your training and teammates to get you through. Make a decision, move forward.

On one occasion when things did not go smoothly, my partner and I became disoriented underneath a large amphibious ship. Not a great place to get lost. We ended up under a pier alongside the ship where we could actually surface and talk (yell) at each other quietly. Since I was the lead diver, the current situation was my mistake, so I actually listened to him when he said "Follow me" and we went back under the water. Twenty minutes later, we ended up at the same spot under the pier quietly discussing (yelling) our situation. At that point, we decided to stay under the pier and surface swim to our target location. Risky, due to all the hazards in the water under the pier, but we were running low on air and didn't have a choice. Once at the aft end of the ship, we slipped back underwater for an easy swim to the rudder, attached the charge, and swam away. That was one of the few times I can remember losing my composure during an operation. Thankfully, it was a training mission and not actual combat. Training missions in the SEAL Teams ended up being as difficult as the real ones. Granted, no one was shooting at you, but mistakes during training often came with an outcome of injury or death. The Navy SEAL Memorial in Fort Pierce, Florida, holds the names of every Frogman who has died in combat or in training for that very reason.

Another dive training mission comes to mind; it really didn't teach me anything I didn't already know but is worth mentioning. Navy Base Roosevelt Roads in Puerto Rico was one of the most beautiful places on the planet to conduct dive training—warm, crystal-clear water, good weather, and plenty of fun. The only thing you had to worry about was bioluminescence, small sea creatures that would light up like a flashlight as you dove by. Virtually impossible to hide in crystal-clear water no matter how deep you are. However, there are always ways to minimize the risk of being seen. On one such night, my partner and I decided to dive under the ships and boats in the harbor in order to minimize the chance of being seen by anyone standing topside. A straight shot in would have produced a virtual arrow of light right at us. The path was definitely the long way around and would add an hour to an already long dive. The ships and boats were all different shapes and sizes; it was a working port. As we made our way to our target, I concentrated on the compass, depth gauge, and watch to ensure we were on time and on course. That is the job of the navigator in a night ship attack. My buddy was supposed to be watching for obstacles and keeping an eye on me. "Rosy Roads" was one of the few places you could actually do that at night without having a hand physically on your partner so you would not get separated. As the time went by, I became even more focused because I knew we were getting close to the target. That is when I went full speed into the head of one of the biggest sharks I had ever seen above or below the water. Luckily, I was underwater when this happened and no one but my dive buddy heard the high-pitch scream that erupted from my mouthpiece. I was fortunate I didn't spit it out of my mouth which would have caused me to surface and face more embarrassment. Once I got my senses back, I realized my buddy was actually belly laughing underwater for some reason. The reason came to me quickly. The shark was actually hanging from the back of a large commercial fishing boat, tail up in the air with its head just deep enough for me to run into it. A typical dive would take place at 10 to 20 feet since we were diving 100-percent oxygen. But, since we were in the harbor, we were at about five feet. Perfect to have a good laugh when not looking around. I regained my composure and made a mental note to screw my friend worse than he had just done to me. We completed the mission and had a good laugh over drinks later that evening. I have had enough time underwater at night to say you do not want to see anything besides your compass and your buddy. The mind starts playing tricks on you. Every shadow is a shark.

Another dive story I would rather forget happened during a training dive in the port of Tunis, Tunisia. Filthy, dirty sewage-polluted ports are the norm in most places that Navy SEALs operate. This was no exception. While working with the Tunisian Frogmen, one of our missions was to train with their diving equipment in case sometime in the future that was the only option to complete our mission. In this case, the rig was made in France and called the Oxyger. Similar to the Draeger Lar V we used, all the basic components were the same—oxygen bottle, chest air bag, and chemical container to absorb your $CO_2$. On this night, I was assigned to an older Vietnam-era SEAL that could still handle just about anything thrown his way. I was at least 25 years younger than he was so I figured I could endure anything coming my way also. Unfortunately, what I didn't know at the time was it was somewhat easy to "over breath" the Oxyger and succumb to what is known as an "$O_2$ hit." Without getting into dive physics, an $O_2$ hit happens when your body absorbs too much oxygen under pressure, many times, causing you to pass out. After about thirty minutes into the dive, I started to recognize the symptoms which are beat into every SEAL's head before every dive. The only problem is you have to listen. I didn't want to look bad in front of one of my heroes. He was a Vietnam-era SEAL with many combat missions under his belt and I didn't want to let him down. I finally was forced to grab him by the arm and give him the "go to surface" signal. Pride is a strange thing. I thought about it a lot while underwater and not once when we went to the surface. I was happy to be alive and alright. I explained to him what had happened while bobbing on the surface as I recovered. He basically looked at me in disbelief, called me a dumbass, and said "Never do that again." So much for pride. If I had done what I had been trained to do in the first place, this would have been a non-story other than I contracted hepatitis from the polluted port water.

Portsmouth Naval Hospital in Portsmouth, Virginia, was no place I wanted to be. When I finally turned a funny-looking yellow color, our SEAL corpsman figured it was time to send me to the emergency room. Sure enough, full-blown Hepatitis A. They gave me some drugs and put me into an open-bay barracks called the infectious disease ward. The only thing separating patients was a flimsy curtain and about four feet. I couldn't move for about a week. It seemed and sounded like people were dying all around me; very disturbing for someone trying to recover. I lied to my parents and told them everything was alright; I was a SEAL after all. When I finally had enough strength to move, I convinced my doctors it was time to release me. I put on a stoic face, got dressed, made my way from the elevator to the front door, and collapsed on a bench right outside the hospital while I waited to be driven to the airport by a friend. I only had to make it back home to Wisconsin where I knew I would really be taken care of and out of the hell that was the infectious disease ward. Thirty days later, I reported back to duty looking forward to my next mission. I needed every one of those 30 days to fully recover.

Diving in Virginia at Little Creek Naval Base was one of the most challenging dive areas I have ever operated in. Every outside factor known to diving had to be contended with—polluted water, jellyfish, cold temperatures, and heavy ship traffic, both civilian and U.S. Navy; Little Creek had it all. My partner and I were one of three pairs training to attack a ship on the far side of the harbor to where we had been inserted. Like anything in the Special Operations world, two is one, one is none. In this case, the odds were that one of the three pairs of combat swimmers would reach the ship and complete the mission. On this day, everything went as planned. We hit the ship perfectly where we intended, attached the simulated mine to the rudder, set the timer, then departed the way we had come in. The path to and from the ship required us to swim across the actual Little Creek channel all the ships going in and out transited. We were about halfway through the shipping channel when we heard a large vessel approaching. The noise was growing by the second. Of course, the dive was at night which meant no light at all. Pitch black. Our procedure in this case was to head to the bottom of the channel below the keel of the ship and let it pass overhead before starting our pre-planned route to the extraction point. The noise was deafening as we headed to the bottom and literally buried ourselves in the mud and muck. It felt like our entire bodies were vibrating from the sound of the ship's engines. The only things not stuck in the mud were our legs and fins, which we were using to kick and get even deeper in the crud. Two minutes later, our blood pressure went back to normal and we continued with our dive. Approximately 30 minutes later, we realized something was wrong. We should have been at our extraction point but did not recognize any of the telltale signs. No lights from piers, no gradual slope from shoreline; it was time to take a peek.

The process of taking a combat swimmer "peek" is complicated. The goal is to spend mere seconds above the water, get a bearing on your target, and get back under the surface to relative safety. First you have to orientate yourself with your compass to make sure you are facing in the right direction for your peek. Once that is complete, you must slowly start rising to the surface in order to use the air in your dive rig so it does not expand at too great a rate that will shoot you to the surface. Many a dive team has been discovered because they did not take the time for that step. Third is to have your buddy ready to pull you underneath once the peek is complete. In this case, that was my job. My buddy went to the surface as planned and I started to count. One thousand, two thousand, three thousand, time to pull. Just as I was ready to pull my partner down, he pulled me up to the surface. Definitely not the plan. It took me a few seconds to orientate myself before I started to look around and see where we were. At first, I had no idea where we had ended up. After about a minute, we realized we were in the middle of Chesapeake Bay and a good two miles from our extraction point. How in the world did we end up there? Boats and ships everywhere moving at all speeds. We did not have enough oxygen left to dive back to the target, so we decided to call in the safety boat with a red flare all SEALs carry on their knives for occasions such as this. The emergency flare had a red glowing end for nighttime and a red smoke end for daytime. My partner pulled his flare from his knife and held it up as high as he could before pulling the ignition tab. Nothing happened. The flare was either old, defective, flooded from the dive, or all three. He threw it in the water. Last flare, last chance before a long night of swimming ahead of us. My flare worked. The safety boat, which by this time thought we were dead, was relieved to see us.

Every dive is briefed and debriefed, as is the custom for most operations. What we found out in this debrief was there had been an extremely large, unscheduled container vessel transiting the channel at the same time we were diving across, thus the mud dive. Turns out there was only 5–10 feet between the ship's keel and the bottom of the channel. We did as trained and hit the bottom and survived. After the ship had passed and we continued our dive plan—plan your dive and dive your plan—the current had shifted with a vengeance and literally sucked us out of the channel and into Chesapeake Bay; a series of events no one could have foretold. We counted our blessings and went back to the locker room to clean off our equipment and get ready for the next evening's dive. As we were cleaning off our gear, my buddy held up one of his fins. There was a large gash in the rubber from the prop of the ship that had passed over us.

Sometimes it is better to be lucky than good.

CHAPTER 8

# Better to Be Lucky than Good

Without standards it is very hard to maintain order and discipline. Without grooming standards, there is no need to get a haircut. Without physical fitness standards, there is no need to work out. Standards are the key to success for any military unit, business, or household. The hard part is selecting standards that are relevant and can survive the test of time with common sense justification. There has to be a reason.

SEALs are required to work out at least five days a week for up to 2–3 hours each day. Everything from swimming to running to lifting and everything in between is acceptable. The absolute worst issue for any SEAL is having a more senior overweight SEAL telling you what to do. If the guy can't even take care of his own body, what makes you think they will take care of you. Insensitive? Correct. Accurate? Also correct. SEALs don't work out to meet a standard, they work out to crush it. Without a baseline, however, who is to be the judge on who is in shape and who isn't? The time to tell is not during training or combat. As a member of a winter-warfare platoon at SEAL Team TWO, I was fortunate to visit all the miserably cold areas on this planet. One such place was Greenland. Not many Americans can say they visited Greenland and only a few SEALs can say they skied from a Defense Early Warning Site in the middle of the continent to the coast in 10 days. I'm not sure who was responsible for this wonderful idea, but at the time it sounded exciting. Fly from a New York National Guard base on a C-130 equipped with skis to a Russian-missile early warning site and then ski to the coast and conduct a typical SEAL exercise of our capabilities. Sounds plausible until you start doing the math; specifically, adding up the weight of all the equipment and food required to make the trek. A typical combat load of 300 rounds of ammunition, magazines, weapons, and vests is about 45 lbs. Tack on to that cold-weather gear such as a tent, stove for melting snow, fuel, sleeping bag, and extra clothing per individual added about fifty more pounds. Then came the Team equipment—radios, extra batteries, explosives, 0.50-caliber sniper rifle and ammunition—for a whopping 300 extra pounds disbursed throughout the team. Each man carried over one hundred pounds on their body in addition to each two-man team dragging a sled with additional equipment in the 75–100-lb range. Better skiers dragged more weight. Skiing across Greenland was a physical and mental test of endurance harder than anything I had accomplished at BUD/S training in Coronado. The only easy day was yesterday.

The center of Greenland is as flat as a pancake. Nothing to see as far as the eye can see. With only map, compass, and altimeter to guide us, we set out on what would be a true test of strength. The first eight days were long and painful. Ski for 8–12 hours a day, set up camp, pass out, and start again. Twenty-four hours of sunlight did not help matters; it never got dark. Sheer exhaustion was the only thing that allowed our bodies to shut down every "night." The key to sleeping in the cold is to have a buffer or ground pad between your sleeping bag and the ice. Without it, you would eventually wake up freezing every few hours. As we were setting up camp one day in a steady 30-mph windstorm, one of my teammates accidentally loosened his grip on his ground pad and it took off like a rocket, never to be seen again. I made the usual comment—"dumbass"—and continued working on my own gear, now being extra careful. I knew the guy would survive, but his life had just become much more difficult. Oh well, no time to dwell on others' misfortune.

There is a happy ending to this part of the story, believe it or not. Approximately 30 minutes after my teammate had lost his ground pad, we saw a blue shape coming from the opposite direction, heading straight at us at high speed. No one realized what it was until it was right on top of the camp. Someone had lost their own ground pad God knows where, in Greenland, on that day and it was traveling toward the camp. No one could believe it and many people I have told this story to don't either. Bottom line, we grabbed the sailing pad and gave it to the guy who had lost his. True story. Sometimes it is good to be lucky.

Day nine brought us to the edge of the Greenland ice shelf, definitely the most dangerous point of the trip with ravines and crevasses so deep you could not see the bottom. One missed step or ski and you were going to be injured or worse. By that time, we were all running low on food. The trip had taken more energy than we had planned for. Knowing this day would be the most critical to survive, we ate most of what we had left and carried on. Somehow, we all made it off the ice. No one fell, no equipment lost. It was a miracle. As we hit solid ground, we were able to finally take off our skis and tie them to our back packs, which were now lighter after we ate all our food. I can remember actually falling asleep as we were walking off the ice looking for a place to set up camp. Thankfully, it was not on the side of a cliff, in case I had stepped the wrong way. We set up camp for the last time to try to get some sleep and prepare for tomorrow's upcoming mission. As Team sniper, it was my responsibility to care for the 0.50-caliber sniper rifle, a beast which weighed a ton but could reach out over a mile to its target. The target in this case was a 50-gallon steel drum about 900 yards away with a can of gasoline on top simulating a radar antenna positioning motor which, when hit, would have stopped the function of the array. It was also supposed to blow up upon impact. Ten days across Greenland, no food left, tired and cold, and the first two shots missed. Had I knocked the scope loose? Had I actually just missed? Devastated, it was mission complete at that time and we headed to the extraction point for warm food, warm showers, warm clothes, and warm drinks. I could cry about my mistakes later. After a few hours, clean clothes, and a full stomach, life was good again. I also found out the rounds had actually impacted the steel drum underneath the gas can but did not set off the gas. Victory. No training or standard could have prepared me for this event. However, everyone has to start

somewhere and the initial screening test for BUD/S is the standard.
SEAL physical screening test:

| Event | Competitive Repetitions/Time | Rest Period |
|---|---|---|
| 500-yard swim using breast and/or sidestroke | 10 minutes | 10 minutes |
| Push-ups | 79 | 2 minutes |
| Sit-ups | 79 | 2 minutes |
| Pull-ups | 11 (dead hang) | 10 minutes |
| 1.5-mile run wearing boots and trousers | 10:20 minutes/ seconds | N/A |

# CHAPTER 9

# If You Are Going to Cheat, Don't

I served at SEAL Team TWO (ST-2) under Master Chief Rudy Boesch for five years before volunteering for ST-6 in the summer of 1985. I never would have had the opportunity if it had not been for a lenient senior leader who gave me another chance. When departing for a six-month winter-warfare deployment, the first stop at the time was a Naval Special Warfare detachment located on a Royal Air Force base in Machrihanish, Scotland—a wonderful place which was always cold and wet with 40-mph winds driving the rain into every orifice you have. It was probably one of the worst environments you could imagine operating in. Temperatures hovered between 30–40 degrees Fahrenheit, usually not cold enough to snow, but wet and cold enough to make hypothermia a real concern. I have seen few places more beautiful and greener than Scotland but that did not make up for the harsh conditions I endured trying to survive there. A typical week, while not on travel to some mountain top in Scandinavia, involved working out, usually a long-distance run, and some sort of water work in the North Sea.

Our time in Machrihanish was fairly brutal so our usual pastime was going to the local pubs to unwind and have fun. Getting to town from the base was a problem. No one joins the Navy to get rich. Money was tight, especially for a young enlisted man. Cabs were expensive and unreliable, so the platoon before us had purchased what we call a "turnover" car, which meant each incoming platoon would purchase and maintain the car and use it during their time in Scotland. The plan was solid except the turnover car left for us would never pass a safety inspection without major work and money to pay for it. This is when I had a brilliant idea to forge a legitimate town safety inspection sticker and place it on the turnover car. The only sticker I could get my hands on to forge belonged to the executive officer (XO) of the detachment. The XO in Navy terms is the second in command behind the Commanding Officer (CO). The sticker happened to be on his motorcycle and not on the inside windshield like all the cars driven in the area. I took the sticker off the bike, copied it, and put it back on the bike. No one the wiser, the plan was perfect. I took my time coloring the sticker to make it look exactly like the real thing. Only the closest of inspections would catch this masterpiece.

After five months of enjoyment using the turnover car, we were nearing the end of our deployment and the return to the USA. One of my friends asked if he could use the car to go to church. Apparently, he had found the Lord. Of course I said yes. While my buddy was in church, unfortunately, the car gained some unwanted attention from some of the local "bobbies" who noticed the sticker was not quite right and waited for the owner to return. Needless to say, I was given up quickly since my name was on the registration. I had broken two of the major standard operating procedures of Special Operations: always operate at night and don't get caught. The reason we had never been caught is because we only used the car to get back and forth from the local pubs. The sticker was very hard to see at night and we never gave anyone a reason to question our credibility. In broad daylight and next to a church was a different story. Maybe the Lord was trying to tell me something, so I went and turned myself in to the local police station and hoped for the best. I am not sure what I expected in Machrihanish, but it was worse—a stone room that looked like it was built 500 years ago, with one 12-inch by 12-inch window covered with iron bars, an old mattress on the floor, and a big iron door that would take a few pounds of C4 to blast through. The police let me sit for about five hours before coming to get me for my appearance before the magistrate. Fortunately, the courthouse was about 50 yards from the jail and two of the biggest bobbies I had seen escorted me to it. They actually held on to each of my arms with their other hand underneath my armpits. They thought I was going to run for it. Actually, they did it for good reason because one SEAL arrested for another misunderstanding had actually bolted, and ran through the fields all the way back to the barracks to get away. My trip to court was uneventful. The magistrate asked if I was guilty of forging the sticker, I said yes, and he asked me how much longer I had in the country. I told him seven days, which was lucky for me because I actually think he would have given me a few days in the slammer. He then asked me how much money I had on me, to which I replied, "About two hundred pounds"; amazingly, the fine was 200 pounds. I handle myself fairly well under pressure, but at that point, I wasn't in the state of mind to lie and give him a lesser number. Two hundred pounds was a small price to pay to get out of there. I paid my fine and was a free man once again.

The only problem with justice when you are in the military is that there are two separate and distinct justice systems when you are on active duty. Civilian, which I had just freed myself from, and Military, Uniformed Code of Military Justice, which I was about to face. There is an old and famous saying among the SEAL Teams: "Bad news doesn't get any better with age." My chain of command was fully aware of what was going on at this point because I told them. No sense trying to hide the news. When I returned from town, I found myself standing before the detachment CO and XO. The XO was out for blood since I had used his motorcycle sticker for the forgery. He basically said my request to go to ST-6 would be torn up and he would make my life miserable. The CO, however, had a different take and let me off. To this day, I have no idea why he did. I even asked him many years later after we had both left the Navy and he said he didn't even remember the incident. In the big picture, I guess the offense was small potatoes compared to what was going on in the world. I did not squander my second chance. After the five hours in the cold, wet jail, I promised myself if I got out of this one, I would never get caught again. Just kidding. I actually used the experience to question future decisions and, so far, it has never failed me. I am grateful to the CO for the second chance that really changed my life and set me back on course. 1. If you are going to cheat, don't. 2. If you do it anyway, don't get caught. 3. If you get caught, own it, face the consequences, and go back to number one.

# CHAPTER 10

# If You Can Dish it Out, You Better Be Able to Take It

Hazing is a dirty word in today's times. Maybe it always was. However, during my tenure as a SEAL it was a way of life. Hazing was part of just about every aspect of being a Navy SEAL. Some good, some bad, and some very bad. The hard truth was that some of my teammates didn't know where to draw the line when it got to the bad and very bad categories. A common harassment for all involved in Naval Special Warfare was to provide the beer or other alcoholic refreshments whenever you accomplished something for the first time. In other words, "first time" could mean anything from first parachute jump to first dive to first time visiting the Navy SEAL Museum. If you were a new guy, you were constantly shelling out the cash to pay for the other SEALs' drinking habits. I consider this hazing on the good side of things. No one was inflicting pain on anyone or anything other than the pocketbook. When special occasions arose, however, the physical abuse escalated quickly from good to bad and sometimes very bad. Special occasions included birthdays, marriages, birth of a child, or many other significant events that happen throughout life. The weird thing about this tradition—which happily was discontinued—was that Team guys very seldom openly shared these significant events with others on their team. Most information was gleaned second or thirdhand, which made it worse for the individual being hazed. Comments like "Don't you trust your own brothers?" or "Did your wife tell you not to tell us?" often came out as selected torture was handed out.

One such event happened to yours truly on my birthday. It just so happened to fall on a Friday with a scheduled beer and BBQ lunch before closing out the week. I am still not quite clear as to how my teammates found out it was my birthday, but before I realized what was going to happen, five or six guys jumped me, pinning my arms and legs while tying my hands and feet together behind my back, all while taking or tearing off my clothes. At the time, there were no females at the Command; perhaps my clothes would have stayed on if there were. Once the takedown was complete, as I lay buck naked in the dirt, the entire Command proceeded to sing "Happy Birthday" to me. I felt so special. Unfortunately, at this point, the hazing was just beginning. After softening me up for about thirty minutes with no contact at all, various guys would walk up and offer me a beer. After getting a few pitchers of beer poured on me, I stopped saying yes to the beer and was grateful it was warm outside. As the afternoon dragged on and the others enjoyed their beer and food, I could sense the crowd getting more rebellious. No longer satisfied with pouring beer on me, a few gentlemen had the great idea to drag me to a pile of Sodasorb behind the diving department. Sodasorb is a granular chemical used for diving re-breathers or SEAL rigs that did not give off any tell-tale bubbles while sneaking around under ships or in ports. The chemical absorbed the $CO_2$ in your breath while the diving rig continuously fed you 100-percent oxygen, thus eliminating the need to off-gas. The downside of Sodasorb is it becomes a caustic chemical when exposed to water. If the diving rig happens to leak, or you leave your mouthpiece open, which allows water inside the rig, there is a great chance you will get a caustic cocktail. The cocktail can burn your mouth, throat, and ultimately lungs if you breathe in enough of it. Laying naked and tied up on a pile of used Sodasorb is no fun. When the water hose came out, I knew things were getting worse. I tried to rest as little of my exposed skin as possible on the pile to prevent chemical burns. I was essentially resting the back of my head, balled up fists and heels of my feet on the pile as long as I could hold it. Someone would always come by and give me a kick so I would fall on my side, but I would immediately get back into the position with least amount of exposure. After what seemed like a lifetime (10 minutes), I could feel my skin start to burn. Luckily, there were a few sane heads in the group; they pulled me off the pile and hosed the remaining chemical off my body. Another 30 minutes later, everyone was tired and ready to go home for the weekend. Actually, all the beer was gone. I was eventually left alone to fend for myself and break loose of the zip ties holding my hands behind my back, which allowed me to free my feet. Party over. This type of occurrence happened almost every week for one reason or another.

One of my favorite hazing stories comes from an event which should be one of the happiest times in your life—getting married. Regular people send out invitations, make announcements, and plan grand affairs. Team guys tended to keep the entire event as private as possible, especially if that SEAL happened to be one of the individuals who took pleasure hazing others. They knew that even the guys who normally did not participate in hazing would make an exception for an instigator of past hazing. Well, it just so happened that one of the worst hazers of all time was soon to be married. What made it even better, he tried to keep it secret, which incited even more people to a little payback. On the afternoon the individual was to leave for the wedding, and ultimately honeymoon, we decided to strike. He put up a fight, but a half dozen Team guys can take down just about anyone. Standard to any hazing ritual at the Team, his clothes were ripped off and he was bound by zip ties with his hands and feet behind his back. The rest of the story is also fairly standard until you get to the end. We had an absolute genius pull out a large master lock with key and actually locked it between our victim's body and scrotum. There was just the right amount of room there to get the shackle in place and lock the lock. There was no way to get the lock off by pulling it off unless you truly wanted to hurt yourself. There was also no way to cut it off because the lock was too close to the skin and other very sensitive areas. To add insult to injury, he was also doused with a special blue dye that was used to dye metal parts for machine work. The dye lasts at least a week no matter how hard you try to remove it. It gave a new meaning to the term "blue balls." We then let him go and proceeded to run away because at this point no one wanted to get into a real fight with the victim. Besides, everyone was laughing too hard. The victim soon realized he was in deep trouble when he was told what happened to the one and only key. It was placed in an envelope and mailed to his soon-to-be-wife courtesy of the U.S. Postal Service (there was a back-up key). The key arrived two days later, well before the wedding. His wife didn't talk to us for quite some time, but even she eventually got over it.

The bottom line on this story is that if you are going to participate in hazing or pranks, you better be able to take the good with the bad. There were many SEALs I have known that didn't know what the term "escalation" meant. If you happened to place a dead rat in their locker, they would in turn take everything out of yours and set it on fire. No one-upmanship there. Story over and prank ended.

Hazing that turns to physical abuse is always unacceptable, the same as a BUD/S instructor harming a student. There is a fine line to both items and crossing it becomes easier the more you do it. That is why senior leaders, whether enlisted or officer, must be held accountable when someone goes too far. It is their job to ensure bad things don't happen. Isn't just being a SEAL dangerous enough? The hazing of the old days has been discontinued for good reason. Times change, attitudes change, people change. It's still funny.

# CHAPTER 11

# When Life Hands You Lemons, Make a Drink

I was getting near the end of my first four-year enlistment and began to think what a life outside the military would be like. I was honored to have made it through BUD/S and into SEAL Team TWO, but it seemed like a life on the road constantly training for something that may or may not ever happen would be a hard life. In addition, military life, especially in the SEAL Teams, is very difficult. Yes, we got to do a whole lot of cool things, but the price paid to do those cool things was quite steep. Low pay, no real missions at the time, and my youth all factored into the decision to re-enlist or get out. I was still undecided on what to do when we were assigned a training mission at a base in North Carolina.

The concept of the op was to insert via Special Boat Unit from Virginia Beach to the Oregon Inlet off the coast of North Carolina. From that point, we would assemble portable and man-carriable Klepper canoes (large two-man kayaks) and paddle for the next two days to the target. The SEAL Teams have a way of making anything that should be fun—like kayaking—into a miserable experience. I have since learned I really don't like doing much of anything for over an hour, especially paddling any type of kayak. We made it to the target approximately forty-eight hours later, stashed the boats, and proceeded to unload all the equipment and explosives we had been carrying to prepare to conduct a demolition raid on a staged camp with a bunch of vehicles.

Planning a demolition raid is complicated and requires practice if you are going to destroy multiple targets at the same time. Each target requires its own tailor-made explosive charge. Custom charges mean you have to carry less explosives to do the most amount of damage. Less explosives equals less weight on your back; every pound matters when trying to move quickly. The next problem is that every charge must go off at literally the same time. Explosive charges that ignite before or after all the other charges in line can affect the entire demolition field by rearranging the placement of charges (knocking them off) or creating a cut-off which means that particular charge doesn't fire at all. Mission failure. Charges are connected together using an explosive called demolition cord, or "Det Cord." Individual charges are tied into a piece of det cord or trunk line which fires all the charges near simultaneously. The cord is made of highly explosive material stuffed into a hollow plastic tube that looks like a small rope and can be wound on a reel.

The target we were going after was well equipped with sensors and cameras, which meant no easy overland travel. This was going to be a classic SEAL operation from the water. The only way in without being detected would be a waist- to chest-deep walk along a very swampy coastline, with approach to the target as close to the water as we could make it. The mile or so patrol was expected to take about an hour, moving slowly and quietly.

As we started our patrol, however, we realized the route was not a sandy beach but a tangled mess of underwater roots and other obstacles in our path that slowed our movement to a crawl. The easy answer would have been to put on our fins and swim the mile, except we didn't bring them. Cardinal sin number one in the SEAL world. We probably could have swum without them, but every man was weighed down with weapon, ammunition, explosives, radios, and the like. There was no choice but to slog it out. I fell into the water at least 500 times that night. Feet caught in roots and every other thing you could imagine. At about the three-quarter mile mark or 300th fall, I had a SEAL epiphany—either I start to enjoy what I am doing no matter how much it may suck or get out of the Navy and move on. I'm not exactly sure how it all happened, maybe divine intervention, but I decided right then and there I was going to stay in the Navy and keep being the best SEAL I could be. It was by no means a cake walk after the decision. I still had another 200 falls to go, but I had gained peace of mind. I had found out what I liked to do and I was somewhat good at it. I thought about a good rum and coke for the rest of the night.

With the decision made, I marched on through the swamp and focused on the mission ahead. We finally did make it to the target about two hours later than planned and proceed to affix various demolition charges to different vehicles and buildings on the site. My job was to attach a charge to the drive shaft of a large truck. As I climbed underneath the truck, I carefully taped the charge to the shaft as securely as I could. I did not want it to fall off because it was also equipped with a mousetrap booby trap which would ignite the charge if someone tried to remove it or drive the truck away. After it was attached, I released a long line attached to the safety pin of the boobytrap so I could safely arm the charge from a distance and not blow myself up. I slowly climbed out and, careful not to pull the line, backed into the swamp. Once the team was ready to go, we lit the time fuse, and I pulled the safety pin for the boobytrap. Nothing blew up. All good. At this point the only thing we could do was to move as fast as we could to get away from the blast and any reaction force that would show up after the explosion. Setting up explosives is not as easy as they make it look in the movies.

# CHAPTER 12

# NAVY—Never Again Volunteer Yourself

In the early 1980s, SEAL Teams TWO and SIX (ST-2 and ST-6) shared the same compound on Naval Amphibious Base Little Creek, Virginia. I knew many of the plank owners (original members) of ST-6 and saw them on a day-to-day basis. I was fascinated by their lack of uniforms, no grooming standards, and their use of pagers. Back in the time before cell phones, pagers were like a badge of honor. They made you feel different and special—or at least that is what I thought. I wanted to be part of that. It was actually a very formal process. I filled out a special request chit asking the ST-2 commander and Command Master Chief (Rudy) in 1985 for permission to try out for ST-6. Your chain of command had to approve the chit before moving on to the next step in the process, which was a formal interview from the ST-6 leadership. I had been a good sailor with three separate deployments under my belt at that point, so they approved the chit.

Since I had never experienced a formal job interview at this point, the next phase was nerve racking. I was brought into the ST-6 compound and found myself standing before the ST-6 Commanding Officer, Command Master Chief, and the Command's psychologist. I was very nervous but managed to answer all the questions satisfactorily until the end. I am sure the three of them did this for all interviewees but, as I was walking out, the shrink asked me, "Petty Officer Kaiser, are you a homosexual?" I stood there frozen. What? After 30 seconds, they started laughing and told me to leave. Had I been accepted? What in the world was going on? I was guided to the quarterdeck and asked to sit down and wait.

This was just as bad as my time in jail in Scotland. After an hour or so, the admin chief came out and said, "Congratulations." I was accepted. I would be receiving orders in the near future to an additional six-month ST-6 training program. I got up and left, happy and excited I had been accepted but also concerned about the unknown. What was training going to be like? What did I have to do? How should I prepare? Back in those days, ST-6 was off the books. There was no one to talk to even if they would have said anything.

In some minds, the word Navy stands for "Never Again Volunteer Yourself." I was happy at ST-2. I was established with good friends and a nice place to live. The joke is, why would you want to keep putting yourself out there since you already enlisted? Maybe I just needed change. Maybe I wanted to challenge myself. I always figured there was no reward without great risk, so I signed up for another six months of grueling training. In theory, I was already a Navy SEAL with over three deployments under my belt at ST-2. In practice, I was starting all over again. Past performance meant very little at ST-6. I was there to learn how ST-6 wanted me to perform. It wasn't exactly BUD/S training again. This time the instructor's main job was to teach rather than weed out the weak. If you failed along the way, however, there would be no tears shed as you walked out the door. This was the real deal. First-class training, equipment, and proven warriors ready to take on the next phase of our careers.

Close quarters battle, or CQB, was the skillset which separated ST-6 from the other SEAL Teams of the time. Our main mission was counterterrorism, which meant hostage rescue, one of the most dangerous missions any unit can attempt. Mission failure is gauged by the condition of the hostages, not by what you do, but by what the enemy does. Success or failure is literally a game of inches and sometimes dumb luck. Everyone was expected to be an expert shot under combat conditions. Training was relentless. Not only did we go to the range every day, we would often include our daily workouts as part of the range time to simulate stress, fatigue, and heart rate. Everyone can be a Frogman on a warm sunny day, so we trained in all conditions, night and day, to prepare for the call. When I was assigned to ST-6, there were about ninety SEALs and 10–20 support personnel at the team. Everyone had to be able to do everything from shooting to maintenance of equipment to daily clean up. There was no one else to do it. Today, there are over a few thousand assigned. I was lucky to know most of them in my tenure. What I miss the most about ST-6 is the laser focus the entire command has on completing the mission. It was an honor to be part of that Team for over 25 years.

Realistic training is one of the keys to success on the battlefield. Live fire using your actual weapon was the norm during all training events. Initial training at ST-6 was no different. Basic weapons safety was ingrained into our heads like nothing else. Accidental discharges, or ADs, were a quick way to get the boot from ST-6. There were countless ways to be released. Another example happened during one of our many CQB runs in the kill house. The kill house is a ballistic box that does not allow bullets to escape in close quarters. The first guy in line entered the room followed by his partner. If you encounter a target, you are supposed to go through it and deal with the threat. Unfortunately, the first guy stepped around the target and kept going. His partner behind him engaged the target and ended up shooting the first guy in the back. Luckily, the number one guy was saved by his body armor. Always good to know your equipment works. Both ended up getting the boot but were allowed to try again during a future class. Brutal. Making mistakes that could cost you or your teammate your life is one thing, but always knowing you are one step away from the door is an entirely different mind game.

A SEAL's main purpose in life is to operate. For the most part, we want the mission no matter what it entails. We train and we fight with that one goal in mind; do whatever it takes to get yourself ready for the next mission. My life at ST-6 for the next 25 years revolved around chasing that mission. One of the unknown facts of life for all SEALs is the constant state of readiness. Once called, you must drive into work within one hour, pack your bags and weapons within three hours, and depart via military aircraft at the four-hour mark. Twenty-five years of that life will change anyone.

The method of choice for recall back in the day were the pagers. If you ask a young person what a pager is nowadays, they will not know what you are talking about. But in days past, they were the bomb. I actually felt special for carrying one. We got an 1800 practice recall every night. The pager became an extension of my body. The only time I did not have it was when we were on the road, which averaged between 150–200 days a year. You can't be a good SEAL sitting at home in Virginia Beach. Luckily, I never spent more than three to four years at any one job while assigned to ST-6. Everything from assaulter to sniper to the training department kept me busy and engaged over my career. My favorite positions were Team Sniper and Sniper Team Leader.

I had learned early on that at six feet three inches tall, and sometimes slow and uncoordinated, up-close hand-to-hand combat would probably not be the best choice for me. Hand-to-hand combat or mixed martial arts were never my strong point. All SEALs are required to become proficient at these skills. I could hold my own, but I regularly got my butt kicked in training sessions. My size, however, did not affect my ability to shoot, move, and communicate as a sniper. That's why I eventually realized that remaining on a regular assault team was probably not the best decision for my future well-being. I decided to move to the sniper team—long-distance shots with minimal hand-to-hand contact with the enemy or teammates.

There are many fallacies that surround SEAL snipers. I will quickly try to debunk a few of the most popular falsehoods. Number one, the best sniper rifle is the one you practice with. It doesn't matter what make or caliber. You are just as dead with a .22 as you are with a 300 Winchester Magnum. Number two, you only shoot what you can clearly identify, unless the enemy is shooting at you. SEALs fight at night. Even with the best optics and night-vision devices, you can only see with that amount of clarity to approximately 100 to 150 yards. Snipers are in place to support the main assault. Shooting your teammates or hostages is not a good thing. Number three, leave the long-distance shots to someone else. Not your job.

CHAPTER 13

# Swim Buddy

Teamwork is also ingrained in the mind of every SEAL starting at BUD/S training in Coronado. "Two is one, one is none" is a motto we live by in the Teams, whether it be equipment or personnel. A swim buddy or shooting partner is the one person you can always count on to pull you out of a mess. He is the one to cover your back without question. My swim buddy had been at ST-6 a year prior to my arrival. He was a good man that took me under his wing when I graduated and was assigned to an assault team.

A typical training day started at 0800 with two hours of physical training—running, lifting, swimming, climbing, etc. At 1000, we usually hit the range and practiced close quarters battle and marksmanship. All live fire, no blanks or paint for the most part. From 1200 to 1300 was rest and lunch and then start back up again with 1300–1600 being more range time or other advanced training. On one particular day, we were practicing four-man room entries in which four SEALs would enter a room and engage all the hostile targets. At this point, we were confident in our skills and knew what we were doing. After reloading our magazines and checking our equipment for what seemed like the 100th run of the day, our four-man team lined up at the door. Not knowing if it was going to be lights on or off, our flashlights were ready to go. Each man had his free hand on the man in front of him with the other hand on his weapon. A squeeze from the back of the line passed forward let the number one man know he was cleared to open the door.

As we entered, I could see it was dark, so the flashlights came on. The initial room was cleared of targets within seconds with double taps to the head or body depending on which was visible. Once clear, myself and another SEAL moved into a small room within the room which had been erected inside the kill house to make movement more complex. Upon entering the room, I immediately engaged a target near the door from about two feet away. Once completed, I heard the range safety officer yell "cease fire" and the lights came on. Not knowing what had happened, the standard operating procedure was to put our weapons on safe, unload, and wait for further instruction. I heard a loud commotion outside the room with people yelling and then, "Everybody get out!" As I was walking out, I could see someone lying on the floor with medics surrounding him. I had no idea who it was or what happened until I walked out of the room. "What happened?" It turns out the bullets I had fired into the target of the second room had passed through the wall and struck my shooting partner, who was now lying on the floor fighting for his life. I felt weak at the knees but proceeded to offload my equipment in a total daze. I didn't know what to say or do. That was my friend. I am not a particularly religious person when it comes to regular visits to church, but I said many prayers that day directly to God asking for his intervention. Unfortunately, my prayers were unanswered; my buddy died in the hospital soon after. The bullets had entered his side through a gap in his body armor.

I will never forget our Commanding Officer (CO) walking into the Team room to brief everyone on what had happened. We had scheduled night parachute operations that same evening which he cancelled; I was grateful for that. Then he got into the meat of the briefing. The bottom line was that the incident was a training accident. No one had done anything wrong. The same scenario was utilized many times for many other training events with no problem. The only issue was there were no ballistic walls inside the inner room, which allowed the bullets to penetrate the wall and hit my partner. Simple and painful as that. The CO was briefing the Team to make sure they understood it was not my fault or anyone's fault this had happened. I didn't realize it at the time, but he was protecting me. He did what any good leader would do regardless of the situation: take responsibility and communicate; answer questions and make a plan so this would never happen again. From that point forward, all walls and partitions inside the kill house were ballistically rated to stop virtually any type of ammunition. I miss my friend to this day and talk to him every morning while walking the dog.

CHAPTER 14

# We Ain't Afraid of No Ghosts

One of the better training sites we had at SEAL Team SIX for quite some time was actually an old derelict ship. SS *United States* had many claims to fame but, most importantly, it still holds the record for the fastest trans-Atlantic crossing by a passenger liner (set in 1952). It was a perfect training vessel for everything from diving, climbing, ship assaults, and sniping. It was our very own cruise liner tied up in the Port of Norfolk waiting to be assaulted over and over again. Assaulting a 990-foot ship with a small group of SEALs is no easy task. Every man must study the blueprints of the vessel in order to get to his individual targets. Clearing each room is not an option, so SEALs move to key areas of the ship and try to take control.

A typical method for getting on board a ship is called a caving ladder. Whether diving or surface swimming, the SEALs hook the ladder to the lowest available spot and begin a long climb on a flexible wire ladder that is about eight inches wide. Technique is everything. All loose gear must be secured for fear of getting caught on the ladder and slowing down the assault. There is nothing worse than slowing down your teammates on a ladder because you forgot to bungee cord your rifle to your body. Even the fittest SEAL can only hold onto a ladder for so long before "peeling off" and hitting a teammate or small boat below. One such night, a friend and boat crew member pulled out an old set of rubber (wetsuit) and didn't notice until we were on site and getting ready to suit up. It was very cold outside, with the water temperature even colder, so entering the water without a wetsuit was not an option. The suit was too small for him. He was a small guy but muscular and the arms no longer fit. On this night, he was assigned as one of the lead climbers with the rest of us behind him. Because we operate at night, it was very difficult to see the hand in front of your face let alone the people above and below you. I remember distinctly hearing a loud splash and thinking that someone is a dumbass below me and would be ridiculed for a possible compromise. Better training than the real thing. As I climbed over the rail and took a cover position, I waited for everyone else to get on board before we commenced our assault. With everyone on board, we took a headcount to ensure we were ready. No one realized up until that point that our lead climber had actually peeled from the ladder and fallen over 75 feet into the water. Everything came to a stop so we could make sure our teammate was alright. As we looked over the side with our flashlights, we saw the climber with an arm through the ladder hanging on and floating to the best of his ability. Luckily, he had no major injures other than his pride. The too-tight wetsuit had actually torn apart upon entry to the water and he was shivering. Somehow, he had managed to fall all that way without hitting another SEAL, or anything else for that matter. Sometimes it is better to be lucky than good. We called over the safety boat, made sure he was picked up, and continued on with the training.

Another encounter on SS *United States* that sticks with me to this day is actually a supernatural tale. The ship contained 693 suites on board. It is a great area for room clearance or close quarters battle training. You could literally train for weeks and never see the same room twice. As we started to clear lower and lower decks of the ship, we noticed the rooms were not as large, which is standard on cruise liners. The higher up you are on the ship, the more you pay and the nicer the state room. The other thing we noticed is that, along with state rooms at the lower levels, we also ran into service-related rooms such as the barbershop and medical clinic. What we did not expect to find, however, was a morgue. There were three or four caskets made entirely of metal, in case of a fire on board, and one small child's casket with the outer lid formed in the shape of a small body. Very creepy. As we continued down into the bowels of the ship, the only light available came from the flashlights attached to our weapons which, in this case, were Heckler & Koch MP5s. I hoped my batteries held up because without light it would be impossible to get out of there quickly. We were SEALs and unstoppable, weren't we?

Then the noises started; soft moaning sounds from in front of us. I clarify that because it would not be beyond someone in the group to make the noise intentionally. After about five minutes of soft moaning, the shadows down the hallway started to shift and move on their own no matter how the light from our flashlights played out. If that was not enough, there was a sudden drop in temperature which seemed to come out of nowhere. Not saying that anyone was afraid, but at that moment we all stopped what we were doing and, in a classic case of group thought, turned around and got out of the space. To this day, I am not sure what I saw or didn't see but there was no need to ever go back down to that space again, especially when there were plenty of staterooms above the waterline with portholes and light. I never looked at SS *United States* the same way again.

No matter how badass you think you may be, there is always someone or something that can kick your butt. I think it is healthy, both mentally and physically, to remember that statement, not to change your decisions, but to give you pause before making them.

# CHAPTER 15

# When All Else Fails, Go to the Water

My time in a sniper team assigned to Task Force *Ranger* in Somalia will forever be etched in my memory. The time we spent in Mogadishu was in many ways a culmination of my training and the entire Navy SEAL lifestyle. We had been recalled for the mission at least three separate times leading up to the ultimate deployment. At the time, our sniper team was supposed to be seen as a gesture of goodwill between SEAL Team SIX (ST-6) and our U.S. Army counterparts. Our inclusion was meant to appease many an ST-6 assaulter who did not get the call. We didn't care, we were going, and that was all that mattered. When we arrived in country, however, we realized we would never be fully accepted or trusted to be part of an Army unit. Their question, and rightfully so, was "Why didn't we take more of our own teammates who we know and train with, rather than these SEALs?"

As it turns out, the Army didn't have to put up with us too long before we were given our first mission. Our team of four was summoned to the quarters of our Commanding General. Not typical at all to have the general hand out orders so we thought we had done something wrong and were being sent back to the States. Seemed a bit extreme just because we were Navy guys. Instead, he gave us a few hours to pack and move to a CIA base located on the airfield. Our mission: move to a CIA safehouse in the middle of Mogadishu and protect CIA personnel and others from any potential Somali attack. We could do that, good deal. We soon realized how naive we were; not only were we the only white guys in town with guns, but we were located in a three-story building in the middle of a very congested section of Mogadishu, making it fairly difficult to hold off any type of organized attack on our position. We decided to take the high ground and make the roof our first line of defense. We were all snipers and would be able to put up one hell of a fight until we ran out of bullets or decided to get the hell out. Any good SEAL will tell you, "When all else fails, go to the water." That was exactly what our plan was. We were about a half a mile away from the Indian Ocean where we could actually swim to the Mogadishu airport and our base if we had to. Better than trying to drive or hoof it back to base through the city. Who knows, maybe we could steal a boat. We set up our little base and proceeded to fall into a routine. Two SEALs were always on the roof awake and on guard. Two were either asleep, eating, or working out to stay in shape. We practiced many different contingency plans in case of attack. Guard duty is boring, but it can become the most stressful job you can have within seconds. I have been fortunate to work with many great agents from the Secret Service and I don't know how they do it. No one I know would take a bullet for another guy intentionally. Our motto is to shoot the bad guy before they can shoot you. There are always exceptions to that rule but, for the most part, we are going down fighting.

One of our duties while stationed at the safehouse was to accompany the agent in charge on trips out in town and provide security for him while he paid off various warlords who were friendly to Americans. The "good" warlords also helped to protect the house we were staying at and were to give us a heads-up should any of the "bad" warlords choose to attack. The bailout plan remained the same: make your way to the water; take the money if possible. No one is going to leave a suitcase full of cash if they can help it. Of course, we would have turned it in anyway. Luckily, we were never attacked during one of these movements. Splitting the force is never a good move, especially when our numbers were so small. Life went on and we did our job for the next few weeks until we got word that one of the paid assets providing information and looking out for us had turned up dead the night before. Time to get out; pack everything you have, leave nothing behind.

It was like a movie: pack your things in the middle of the night under the cover of darkness; load up all the equipment and personnel into a piece-meal convoy; and drive a few miles to an abandoned soccer field for helicopter extraction. The road all the way back to the airport had become too dangerous at this point. We waited for the birds to get close and then marked the landing zone with infrared lights in an area big enough to land two Black Hawks at once. The entire operation took 20 minutes to pull off, which is a huge failure when trying to get in and out of an at-risk area, but that wasn't our call. The SEALs were positioned in the stands in order to have clear fields of fire should anything happen. Luckily, nothing did, probably because it was the middle of the night and all the fighters were high on khat, the drug of choice for the Somalis (I found it interesting that drugs could always be found even when food could not). The extract went smoothly, and we landed back at the Task Force *Ranger* compound at the Mogadishu airport. Of course, there was no one there to meet us so we grabbed our gear and started walking to where we thought everyone had set up camp. It didn't take long to stumble across a few hundred of our closest U.S. Army buddies. Fortunately, we ran into a few of our Air Force combat controllers and pararescue friends that set us up with spare cots to get some rest for the night. Tomorrow was a new day and totally new mission.

Well, when life gives you lemons, make lemonade or something like that. We decided to make the most of our time knowing we would not be included in any of the main mission planning or actual work. SEALs, if nothing else, are resourceful and think in the gray area most of the time. When we saw helicopters flying every night that belonged to the 10th Mountain Division and were not part of Task Force *Ranger*, we had to check it out. As fate would have it, one of the pilots from the 10th Mountain was a former SEAL who left the Navy in order to fly helicopters. He also happened to be flying a mission called "Eyes over Mogadishu" which basically put snipers in the air over the city each night to quell any violence directed at the airport where most U.S. forces were staying. Perfect job for trained ST-6 snipers who conducted this type of training regularly with night-vision and laser-equipped sniper rifles. All we had to do at this point was talk our Army chain of command into letting us participate. As it turned out, it wasn't hard at all. The 10th Mountain had been using snipers equipped with Barrett 0.50-caliber sniper rifles that are hard to shoot and control on the ground let alone in an aircraft. The shock wave inside the helicopter must have rattled the pilots pretty good each time the weapon fired. Our weapon of choice for this mission was an old school M14 with laser and optics. Accurate, easy to maneuver, and plenty of knockdown power. Now we get to the Rules of Engagement (ROE), something every Special Forces member knows very well. I'm not sure when they started, I only know I have dealt with them my whole career. True professionals learn to deal with the ROEs and adapt. People outside the circle view them as an unnecessary interference from politicians rather than military leaders. Regardless, we wanted the mission. The ROEs for the "Eyes over Mogadishu" mission were straight forward. You could shoot if someone was shooting at you or setting up to shoot at American forces. It was common to be mortared at the airport on a regular basis. If you happened to catch an enemy mortar team in the open, they were fair game. Typical shot was 100–200 yards max, at night. This was a city, missed shots and collateral damage were unacceptable. We did our job and we did it well; so well in fact that, after two weeks flying the mission, our Army counterparts were concerned we were causing poor morale since we were going out every night and accomplishing something while they mostly sat around waiting for the big raid. That was their job, not ours. It didn't matter, we were scrubbed off the "Eyes" mission and actually given a role in future raids into the city. Win/win.

A direct-action raid is a very complex mission when dealing with different types of aircraft, ground convoy coordination, and different units from different services. Good training and practice are key to success. Since we were no longer flying with the Army, our job was now basically to support our Army counterparts as they conducted the assault operations on whatever the target happened to be that day. What does that mean? We would drive an unarmored HMMWV (High Mobility Multipurpose Wheeled Vehicle, better known as a "Humvee") from the Mogadishu airport to the target site in a large vehicle convoy. The helicopters would go in first to gain the element of surprise followed by groups of soldiers, via ground, assigned to set up security around the target site. Our specific job was to drive directly to the target, set up and wait for any runners the Army would flush out, and check any outbuildings near the main target. Driving the streets of Mogadishu is no easy task. No street signs, no GPS, no real structures that weren't falling in the road, if you could call them roads at all. The roads were mainly narrow dirt paths which sometimes would only be wide enough for one vehicle at a time to pass. Our small part of the convoy consisted of two vehicles: three SEALs and one Army guy in one HMMWV and me and three Army guys in the other in order to better communicate between the units. It was always our standard operating procedure to carry all our equipment in the HMMWVs, including extra water, ammunition, and night vision, no matter what time of day it was. Unfortunately, not everyone did the same and it turned out to be a huge issue as the upcoming battle progressed from day to night and back to day again.

As we drove into the target area, we immediately began to receive incoming small-arms fire, which was expected, but perhaps a bit heavier than we had received on previous missions. As we took up our final positions, the fire increased and we were forced to exit our vehicle and take up cover anywhere we could find it. I ended up in an alleyway with another SEAL exchanging gunfire with some Somali fighters when my teammate was struck in the leg by either a bullet or fragmentation. He went down and called for help. I immediately laid down a base of fire so I could move to his position and assist him. When I moved the approximately twenty yards, I had a thought. It is weird what you think about sometimes in the midst of battle, at least for me. I had carried two fragmentation grenades on my battle vest for as long as I could remember. I had never used one before other than on a controlled explosive range back in the United States. This was my chance. I looked down at my wounded coworker, let him know what I was doing, and made sure we had enough cover to protect us from my own grenade. Messing with grenades is a serious business. I had heard stories of guys accidentally dropping their grenade at their feet or forgetting to pull the pin. I was determined not to let that happen to me. There are actually two safety devises on fragmentation grenades. A safety clip, which we had removed before leaving on the mission, and the actual pin, which you pull, that releases the spoon, giving you four seconds before it explodes. The grenades themselves are heavy, about 14 oz, or nearly a pound, and must be secured to your vest so they don't fall out. I carefully released the tape I had holding the grenade to my vest, pulled it out of my vest, put the spoon portion of the grenade in the palm of my hand and, with the other hand, prepared to pull the pin. The entire action I described above seemed a lot longer than reality (which was probably thirty seconds). I was now ready to go. I took one last look down the alley—nothing worse than fragging your own people—pulled the pin and then remembered, this is not like a baseball. You can't just chuck a hand grenade without throwing out your shoulder. Do I throw underhand? The alley was narrow. What if it hits something and bounces back? I would have to expose myself to throw overhand and who really knows how far it would go. I went with underhand. Low with little arc and hoped it would roll like a bowling ball down the alley. That's what I did. Once it released from my hand, I ducked back behind cover and waited for the blast which happened right about four seconds later. I had always been taught that if you can see an explosion, it can see you which meant, if I was watching, there was a chance I could frag myself. Not going to happen. However, because I didn't watch, it really became anti-climactic. I had built up this moment in my mind only to be disappointed. Oh well, at least it created enough dust in the air to allow us to get out of the alley.

As the battle went on, the enemy had a say in the outcome of the fight and we lost two U.S. Army Black Hawk helicopters to rocket-propelled grenades (RPG), a very basic weapon which could be produced for around a buck fifty each as opposed to the U.S. military version which cost $10,000 each. Funny when you think about it. We found ourselves back at the base to regroup, reload, and prepare to return to the city where others from our force were trapped with no way out. Nothing for granted this go around. We took as many supplies as we could in our still unarmored HMMWV. Everyone was ready to go. We were going to rescue our friends and get them the hell out of the city. Wait, I had to go to the bathroom. I figured this was the time to do it. Going in your uniform is always an option, but who wants to ride in that all night, and the smell. Forget it. I grabbed my weapon and hit the porta-potty. Do you think they had bathrooms with running water in Somalia?

Job completed, I walked back to our HMMWV only to find everyone had shifted seats, leaving only one open for me. The driver's seat is the worst position you could find yourself in. There are two major problems. One, you have to pay attention to the road and other vehicles, not the bad guys. Stopping at an alley intersection was death. Two, I couldn't use my weapon while driving. No chance to shoot back. I had a major leadership challenge in front of me. Take the driver's position and the consequences or tell one of the more junior guys to switch with me. Really not an option in my world; you cannot lead from the front if you are unwilling to do any of the jobs before you. Yes, leaders cannot be all things to all people but, in this case, we were all equal regardless of rank. We had a job to do and we were a small part of a much larger convoy heading back into the city to rescue our trapped teammates. We left the relative safety of the Mogadishu airport and immediately began taking fire. I actually believed the Somalis would think twice about attacking the convoy since we now had four Pakistani M60 tanks, 14 Malaysian armored personnel carriers (APC), 12 HMMWVs armed to the teeth, and one unarmored HMMWV with a few SEALs and Air Force guys that I was driving. Unstoppable. What did stop the convoy, actually, were the Pakistanis and Malaysians. The Pakistani tank commanders thought it was too unsafe for their tanks to enter the heart of the city. Really? The Malaysians wanted troops on foot in front of their APCs to protect them from RPGs. Really? Once the deal was made that we were actually going to do this, the convoy started moving forward again without the tanks. As I drove up to one of the tanks that night, I wondered what it would be like to be inside that beast. Then the turret started moving. Surely, he wouldn't fire with our HMMWV 10 feet away. That is exactly what the tank did. We were all blind and deaf now, hoping no one would start shooting at us. After 30 seconds, our sight recovered and the guys behind us were yelling for us to move. No time to dwell on that one so we kept going. As we made it to our target, our job was to take up a security position which would allow the medics and extraction crew time to get everyone out of their temporary homes in the city. Small-arms fire was constant. I remember looking at one of my guys and watching him follow a goat with his rifle scope. The goat had apparently gotten lost in the battle and was trying to find its way out. It is weird what you think of in times like that. I actually thought he was going to shoot the goat, so I yelled at him not to do it. He looked at me with a grin and moved on to another target. With everything else going on that evening, I was thinking about a goat. Go figure. The goat survived as far as I know. Later that night, we recovered all our trapped teammates and began to move them to a safe area out of the city. Returning to the airport was not an option due to the number of bad guys set up and waiting for our return so the decision was made to travel to a nearby Pakistani-controlled soccer field. Unfortunately, the rescue operation had taken much longer than expected and we could all see the sun was coming up quickly. Daylight meant more engagements with the enemy. Everyone was in a hurry to get the hell out of there as soon as we could. The problem with rushing is that mistakes are made at a time you least want any misstep. We loaded up our HMMWV with as many stragglers as we could and took off with the rest of the convoy. Unfortunately, again, some of the soldiers were left behind in the city and had to run for the stadium. Now we affectionately refer to that debacle as the "Mogadishu mile." Running a mile in full equipment while being shot at is quite the accomplishment. By the time the convoy realized what had happened, it was too late to turn around to retrieve the runners. As we sat in the stands and looked down at the soccer field, the scene was surreal. Medical tents, people running, helicopters landing and taking off with injured, stretchers with fallen warriors. Until that point, we were not fully aware of the actual cost of the battle to our teammates, with 18 killed and 75 wounded out of a little over 100 in the beginning. A Pakistani soldier walked up to us at that point and offered us some soup. We were grateful for the distraction and accepted. We waited for another hour or so for our turn to return to the airport via helicopter. The vehicles could sit for a day or two before being driven back the long way. I was tired of the HMMWV anyway.

One of the best things we did when we returned was to write down some lessons learned from the experience. Memories and lessons have a way of disappearing or changing over time. The best way to capture that valuable information is to write it down or conduct a debriefing with your team to exchange ideas and lessons, which typically happened at the Team bar with a beer in hand when back home. Then, if you are really squared away, someone else can write it down. The biggest historical lesson learned during my time in Mogadishu was "Never fly helicopters within small-arms range in the daytime." This lesson had been learned in blood the hard way from Korea to Vietnam and beyond. Lessons are forgotten without someone reminding you constantly. Remember, everyone wants the mission. It is easy to place blame on politicians or senior leaders when things go bad. We were ready for battle and we dished it out much worse than we received. The enemy has a say in every battle. That just happened to be the day they decided to fight. I do not believe they had a particular hate for Americans; I think they just wanted us out of their country no matter how good our intentions were.

I ended up remaining in Somalia for a few more weeks with hopes of follow-on operations to clean up some of the mess, including the rescue of an Army pilot who was captured by an anti-U.S. clan in the heart of Mogadishu when his helicopter crashed. His co-pilot and two U.S. Army Special Forces soldiers were killed soon after the crash by small-arms fire from the hostile mob who surrounded the helicopter. The intelligence or location of the pilot never came so, once again, we ended up training for contingencies and biding our time for the next move. I found myself a little jumpy after the big battle, especially when there was a loud unexpected noise. It didn't last for long, but I consider myself fairly lucky for coming out of that fight in one piece mentally and physically.

One such explosion took place right in the middle of our compound soon after the battle of Mogadishu. I remember vividly how I was sitting on my U.S. Army-issued cot talking to a friend when, all of a sudden, a large "boom" went off about fifty yards from me. The lights were immediately turned off and everyone was scrambling for flashlights in the pitch black. Was this an attack? As it turns out, the Somalis had launched a mortar round at our compound and had gotten very lucky because it hit right in the center of a group of four or five soldiers who were discussing Task Force *Ranger's* next move. One of those soldiers died from his wounds, leaving all the others in critical condition. Bad day for our side. The Somalis had been launching mortar attacks on our compound on a regular basis. Fortunately for us, they were not accurate at all except on this one occasion.

As time rolled on, it became apparent the U.S. no longer had the political will to fight. It was time to leave. However, like all things in the military, it takes no time to deploy to a fight but an unbelievable amount of time to redeploy. Even though I had thoughts of hanging up my fins, I remembered my training. Never make any decisions while deployed; wait until you are at home for at least two weeks before making your next move. We were all depressed due to the loss of so many Americans. All we wanted to do was fight or get out. I guess at that point in my career I realized the only people you can count on are the guys to your left and right. No one else is going to look out for you like your teammates. They are the only ones that are in it with you.

# CHAPTER 16

# Boring until It Isn't

My days as a SEAL sniper really changed over the years. Being a good shot has always been important, but the additional skills needed to perform at a high level changed with the advancement of technology. Radiomen in the 1980s and 1990s learned Morse code. Snipers learned how to stalk their targets using cover and concealment dressed in specialized ghillie suits (camouflage sniper clothing).

Fast forward to Bosnia, where I was the senior enlisted SEAL for a group of snipers in the late 1990s and early 2000s. Like most wars, religion had a major role in how the conflict started. In this case, it was Muslims fighting the Orthodox and Catholics. I have always said that without religion I would have been out of a job. Not that far off when you really think about it. After four years of major fighting in the region, hostilities were greatly reduced and a shaky peace was kept by a United Nations peacekeeping force. SEALs don't typically deploy anywhere to keep the peace but, in this case, there was a large group of "people indicted for war crimes" still running around the region who needed to be caught and sent to the Hague to stand trial. Great sniper job. Find the bad guys and support the assaulters when they came in to capture the individual.

I rolled into Bosnia on my first four-month deployment in 1999 as the senior enlisted leader for a large sniper team which included SEAL snipers and Navy support personnel in addition to other service technical support. It was quite the eye opener for me and a chance to make a difference in a place that had really suffered. Some of the atrocities these people were being charged with were beyond evil. In order to catch these guys, we had to try to blend in, which is not an easy thing to do for a bunch of knuckle draggers. Bosnia was one of the only places where SEALs like me could actually fit in and not draw unwanted attention as we were doing our job in a foreign country; light-skinned, tall, well-kept folk for the most part who would not notice us as long as we didn't have to talk. There were also plenty of Americans around in different capacities, from military to contractors to non-government organizations. In order to fit in, we quickly learned most Bosnian males between the ages of 20 and 40 had longer black hair below the ears or even shoulder length. There was no way I was going to color my hair at the time, although it would have been a good idea, but I was willing to let it grow out. With the lessons I had learned from Rudy back in the early days, this was not going to be easy. I actually lasted an entire month before I broke down and went to the barber. I realized then I was not cut out for undercover work and would rather be in the field trying to track someone down than in the city trying to blend in. I was fortunate my job did not require the kind of close personal interaction with the locals required of the rest of the operators.

Headquarters came up with a somewhat believable cover story and then we were off to the races. Very slow races. Surveillance work is boring until it isn't. Ninety-five percent of the time is spent sitting around and freezing your butt off in the dirt. Only in the movies do you get a nice building of some sort with a window to observe out of. It's not exactly that we were hated by the Bosnians, but no one wanted to be associated with the U.S. military, especially when we all knew our presence wouldn't last and then they would have to answer for their actions.

The closest I got to the locals was actually paying the rent for the various storage warehouses and living accommodations. One such warehouse was owned by an older Bosnian gentleman who made me drink with him to the point of being drunk every month. I'm not sure if he knew we were U.S. military, but we came up with many elaborate stories to let him know we were legit and would pay our bills anyway. I was never quite sure if I could trust the gentleman, so I made sure to check my sidearm and let everyone know where I was going and what

I was doing. Neither probably would have helped much if he truly was a bad guy, but it helped me feel better.

The warehouse became our main base for planning and the storage of vehicles and equipment, and my home for the duration. Not very pleasant, but we cleaned it to the best of our abilities. Also included in our team were incredible Navy Seabees that constructed a secure space for all our communications equipment.

Sniper teams would come in for their daily assignments, restock with water, food, and batteries, and hit the road all over the country looking for our targets. The beauty of running an operation is that you get to make the decisions. Between my Officer in Charge (OIC) and myself, we had it. We called the shots depending on intelligence, experience, and input from our sniper teams. Sounds glamorous for a military guy, but it isn't. Most of our day was making sure the teams had everything they needed. Logistics are the life blood of a successful op, not to mention morale. News from home and food and drink are critical. Things like a proper functioning toilet with toilet paper can make a world of difference when most of the houses the sniper teams were staying in were hit and miss. Our base became a locker room for showers and hygiene, unfortunately, with only one person to keep it clean. I couldn't let the officer do that type of work. The Master Chief once again became the bathroom and toilet cleaner. Nasty work, as I am sure you can imagine. SEALs aren't known for their cleanliness. They probably even enjoyed making a mess knowing who was cleaning it up. Oh well, life in the Teams. King one day, pawn the next.

That was a great deployment. I had a great OIC and a very qualified group of SEAL Team SIX snipers focused on doing their best to find these scumbags. When it was time for an actual operation, such as a reconnaissance mission or snatch, my job would change to more hands on and briefing the chain of command with the OIC. It was very sad to see a once-beautiful country like Bosnia, a country that had actually hosted a recent Winter Olympics, reduced to rubble from years of war. Our mission there was noble, but it is never a good idea to send in the military to conduct police business. That is what we were doing—trying to locate and arrest war criminals to stand trial in the Hague. This was probably the last time I felt I could have fit into a foreign country and mingled with the locals.

Patience and persistence were the key words in Bosnia. Never give up and eventually your long hours of observing a target will get you the information needed to launch the operation. Focus on the task at hand and try not to think about the upcoming weeks and months ahead of you.

# CHAPTER 17

# Everybody Works for Somebody

As your time rolls on in the military, you either move up, move out, or become irrelevant. I was lucky enough to move up and take on more senior management roles. One such role was the lead training chief for SEAL Team SIX (ST-6) in 1995. I was responsible for all training conducted by, and for, the new guys coming into the Team along with the advanced training for the SEALs already assigned to assault teams. It was a great job, but it involved a lot of traveling. It is impossible to be a good SEAL in Virginia Beach. You have to go to where the training is; training at home is a luxury. The time not to screw up is when you are going through an initial training course. As the training chief, it was my job to give the bad news to guys who were not going to make it through training. That job really sucked. I tried to put myself in their place and imagine how I would have felt if I had been canned—not good. Most knew it was coming; I was the one making it official.

I typically did not get involved with managing the initial physical screening test for guys in order to start training. On one occasion, I was asked to help out and monitor the sit-up portion of the test. It just so happened the guy I chose to watch actually cheated on the test and recorded a number higher than what he performed. Black and white decision here. He cheated, was caught, and was shit-canned immediately, or so I thought. Everyone works for somebody, unless you happen to be independently wealthy. In all cases, I worked for the Commanding Officer (CO) of the SEAL Team. Apparently, the CO was under pressure to produce more qualified SEALs from his boss at U.S. Special Operations

Command in Tampa. Not being aware of the policy, I automatically got rid of the guy and was immediately overruled by the boss. Nothing personal, that is just the way it is. No grudges or hurt feelings. Move on and deal with it. As it happens, the guy ended up having a good career.

Knowing when to pick your battles is an art form. Everyone is replaceable. When you start thinking you are indispensable to the team, it is easy to make bad decisions. I'm not saying you cannot be passionate about a cause but, when it becomes emotional, reason is often lost. SEALs are very good at compartmentalizing their emotions during times of high stress. With that skill, we pay a high price during low-stress periods with drinking and other unhealthy habits. Drinking to relieve stress has been a part of the culture of the SEAL Teams since I joined. Like everything in life, some guys can handle the stress and some can't; that is what really differentiates a good SEAL from a great SEAL—the ability to perform in combat and then as a regular citizen at home. If I really wanted to push for the sit-up cheater's firing, I could have, but for what purpose other than my own ego. Dwelling on items you have very little control over is a distraction from your mission. Move on and take up the next challenge.

I like to think of myself as a good SEAL. I know it doesn't sound very modest, but if you don't have that mindset, like most of the SEALs I know, why would you want to be a SEAL in the first place. Belief in yourself and your abilities is paramount to success. Thinking you are equal to, or better than, your teammates helps keep you motivated to stay on top, put in the extra time, and stay that way. Testing your skills is critical. Belief in yourself is not good enough, you have to prove it every day; similar to the Navy SEAL Ethos—"Earn your Trident every day."

I was lucky enough to participate in what was essentially a Special Operations Olympics called the Combat Team Competition on four separate occasions. The event was hosted by the German GSG-9 in Bonn, Germany, and was attended by Special Forces units from around the world. British, Australian, German, Austrian, French, U.S. Army, to name a few, all attended to compete. The team consisted of five men with one alternate. We had high hopes of winning on each of the four occasions I competed. We never won the overall title. The competition consisted of ten standalone events with shooting, climbing, driving, hostage rescue, swimming, etc., which each team had to complete, usually on the clock. There is no better way to test your abilities than to compete against the very best. The competition was held every two years.

When an invite came into the Command, a notice was put out to all the SEALs for tryouts. For some reason, which I found hard to understand, only a handful of guys would show up and they were usually the same individuals that competed in previous competitions. We had world-class athlete SEALs at ST-6 but, for some reason, most wanted no part of the competition. I didn't figure out the problem until my third time competing when I was trying to recruit a strong competitor to join us. He said, "You guys never win. Why would I set myself up to fail?" Wow, was that the reason? They didn't want to lose. Yes, it sucks to compete and lose. We never won the overall title, but we did win or place in many of the individual events against some of the best teams in the world. We tried our best and that was good enough. Not competing or trying because you may lose is not the way to become better at your profession. No one died and no one got hurt. We learned valuable skills for the future, we licked our wounds, and moved on to do it again in two years. The other intangible in the competition was the invaluable number of friends and contacts made. Should you find yourself on the battlefield with one of these other units, you had an immediate relationship and knowledge of their skillsets and abilities. Play the long game. Unfortunately, many of my own teammates didn't see it that way.

CHAPTER 18

# Risk and Reward

SEALs are tested on a daily basis in many ways. As the saying goes, "Earn your Trident every day," or live up to your reputation every day. One of the testing methods more related to actual SEAL skills was called Tasks, Conditions, and Standards. Usually written up by the training department, these were a set of standards to test your individual and team skills. The tests were as close as you could get to combat without getting shot at. Similar to the Combat Team Competition, I loved them, but many others did not. As a member of the SEAL Team SIX sniper element, long-range shooting was our specialty. The very first shot of the day, or "Cold Bore," was the most difficult because you had to judge all factors that would determine whether you would hit the target or not. Things like temperature, wind, and distance all had to be exact in order to hit a target over five hundred yards on the first shot. The sniper test was fairly basic. You had two minutes to get into position, determine the distance of the target, determine wind speed, temperature, and all the other factors that affect your bullet's trajectory, and fire to hit a man-size target in the kill zone.

On one occasion, my four-man sniper team had a no-notice test in which we were recalled to the Command to perform. We packed up our equipment and drove to a plane which took us to Fort Bragg, North Carolina, to conduct the test. New area, new range, and out of state—a real test. Standard was the same. Two minutes. Go. Each SEAL sniper grabbed his weapon, laid down, and got to work. My target happened to be at approximately 800 yards with a very light left to right wind. I made my calculations and fired. Now was the hard part: waiting for the results. I had a good hit slightly right of the kill zone of the target but still a good killing shot in reality. I thought I had failed the test and was very disappointed. What I didn't realize was that was not what our commanders were thinking. We had just done quite a remarkable job. No-notice recall, fly to another state, shoot cold bore, and get the job done, at 800 yards no less. They were pleased in what we had accomplished. Although not perfect, pretty darn close. I learned a lot about myself and teammates that day which I never would have if we had not tested our abilities in the most realistic ways possible. Embrace the stress, pressure, and practice and you will no doubt come out on top in the real world.

One of the other tasks the snipers were given on a regular basis was to conduct capabilities demonstrations, or "dog and pony shows" as we liked to call them. Many would look at these events as distractions or a waste of time. A typical "show" could last up to three days if we had to travel to Fort Bragg or Tampa. The snipers tried to use this task as an opportunity to hone our skills. Failure is not an option in front of high-ranking civilian dignitaries and military officers. Not only could we not fail, but we took it up about 10 notches. A typical sniper could hit a one-inch by one-inch square at 300 yards without question. So, we came up with the idea of having our Commanding Officer (CO) stand next to balloon at approximately 100 yards on the rifle range. Of course, we practiced this regularly, but when the CO was standing next to the target, try to imagine the instant pressure and stress each sniper had to endure. Typically, we used two snipers for each target just like the real world when we had the manpower. The announcer would talk about a typical hostage-rescue scenario to get the crowd revved up and then the CO would reach for his radio and give the actual order to fire. The balloon would pop and the CO would walk back to the crowd and explain what just happened. Another demonstration we liked to do was to have a target sitting in the back seat of a four-door vehicle on the rifle range. The snipers would set up at the 200-yard line and wait for the vehicle to drive in front of them. With a simulated stop sign, the vehicle would stop and the snipers would fire, hitting the target in the

Future Navy SEAL? Author aged two and on the right path. Thanks Mom.

The first Joint Warrior. Author aged six. Someone tried to influence my decision-making with a U.S. Army uniform. I saw the light.

Sniper and Breacher training. Salton Sea, California, circa 1988. Notice the old school M14.

Winter Warfare SEAL Team TWO. Narvik, Norway, circa 1983.

Greenland icecap, circa 1984. Long-range navigation from Defense Early Warning Site to coast.

On patrol. Winter-warfare training at Goose Bay, Labrador, Canada, circa 1984.

Winter-warfare training with Norwegian Jaegers at Tromso, Norway, circa 1984. Notice the broken ski pole taped with two sticks.

Sniper training, Fort A.P. Hill, Virginia, circa 1983. Homemade ghillie suit to blend into foliage.

September 1993. Standing watch downtown, Mogadishu, CIA safe house. Again with the M14.

October 1993. After the battle of Mogadishu, getting ready to go back out. Changed over to an M4 to fit in the HMMWV better.

SEALs on the water, circa 2023, for a Navy SEAL Museum action video.

SEAL swim pair on rebreathers. The lead diver is using an attack board for navigation.

BUD/S trainees getting crushed by a wave in an IBS (Inflatable Boat Small). Who would have known these are the same boats that were used by the original Frogmen of WWII Naval Combat Demolition Units.

Author getting ready to lead a Swim Out ceremony.

Memorial Day 2023, Navy SEAL Memorial. No kneeling here.

Navy SEAL Museum Muster. Swimming out our Fallen.

Frogmen getting ready to swim out the ashes of our fallen brothers. This picture was taken in front of the Navy SEAL Memorial located on the grounds of the National Navy SEAL Museum.

Navy SEALs swimming out the ashes of our brothers on Veterans Day.

The author and the chaplain during the ceremony. The author is in the tiger stripe camouflage uniform in honor of our Vietnam veterans.

The author leading the team back to the families after the release of the ashes.

Barbara and Rick Kaiser at Palm Beach Navy SEAL Evening of Tribute in support of both the Navy SEAL Museum and Navy SEAL Foundation. April 2022.

back seat and leaving the driver and passenger unscathed. We couldn't afford to replace vehicle windows every time we did this drill so the windows were rolled down.

If you really think about the last two examples of a capabilities demonstration, you should probably be thinking "What in the hell were you thinking?" Any slip would have caused the death of the person next to the balloon or sitting in the vehicle. True, but on the other hand, can you imagine the confidence you must have in your men and teammates to be the one down range of those snipers? Unbelievable. During practice sessions, we regularly took turns acting as the CO or driver. Then we all knew exactly what it was like to be on the receiving end of that situation. We never missed and no one ever balked at going down range. Talk about a confidence builder under a huge amount of stress. That is what gets you ready for war.

The snipers were not the only ones performing. We also conducted live-fire displays with living, breathing people in the "kill house." Usually, one of the dignitaries that would not pass out was sat in the middle of the house along with the CO to watch the demo. Each had ear and eye protection along with about six to eight bad guy targets all around them. When the signal was given, an actual explosive charge would blow the door off and four SEALs would burst in the room and engage the targets. All done in five seconds. The CO's only job was to place his hand on the dignitary's leg to keep them in place should they panic and decide to get up and run out of the place.

Of course, all things come to an end. Eventually the team hired a "High-Risk Safety Manager." I think we gave the guy a heart attack when we tried to explain exactly what we were doing and why. He was not happy and convinced the CO to stop any live-fire demonstrations with human beings. Probably not a bad call, but training like that cannot be replicated in any other way.

I get a lot of questions about rifles, scopes, caliber of ammunition, and anything in general related to long-distance shooting. I have done it for quite a while and consider myself a fairly good shot. The fascination with long-distance shots has always confused me. Guys talk about 1,000-yard shots and further like it is the equivalent to the Holy Grail. I suppose if you look at the skill as an ultimate challenge, I can get behind it, but, as a military option, it is just not practical. As a U.S. military sniper, you are given great independence to complete your mission as you see fit. With that independence comes great responsibility based on morals and ethics.

It is your responsibility to ensure that, when you pull the trigger, the bullet is going to strike your intended target and that the specific target you are firing upon deserves their fate according to your rules of engagement (ROE). Many people complain about ROE and how it hamstrings our troops more than the enemy. In some cases that may be true but, in most cases, strict ROE help define your actions when the whole world is blowing up around you in combat. Every move that is made is reviewed by military lawyers before and after the mission. It is now part of life. You deal with it and move on if you want to be part of the mission. If not, go home and find another profession. Realistic training is key. Whether real world or training, you must follow the same guidelines and briefings when it comes to ROE and legal briefings. After a while, it becomes second nature and no one complains. Order and discipline are a good thing when things go bad.

There are simple rules to live by as a sniper: 1. Know who or what you are shooting at. You can't pull the round back once fired; 2. Minimize collateral damage. This comes into play when dealing with civilians or the possibility of civilians nearby; 3. Protect your teammates.

Number one is not possible when shooting at long distances unless your ROE is to shoot anything that moves or anyone holding a weapon. I have never been given that ROE or know anyone who has. Any SEAL will tell you "everyone" carries a weapon in a war zone. If we went to war in Florida right now, three quarters of the population would be legitimate targets under that ROE. This is where the morals and ethics come in. Why is it impossible to hold to number one at long distances? You can't see the target. No matter how good your optics are, you may see a blur of a shape of a human being. Is it a man? Is it a woman? Is it a child? Doesn't matter—if you can't identify it, you can't shoot. There is always the exception to the rule, like the target is shooting at you or other friendlies, but, typically, SEAL snipers are not in the field during that sort of mission. SEALs and all Special Forces operate at night. The best night-vision capability on a rifle will get you a clear picture at a maximum of 200 yards on a good night. In addition, an average engagement by any soldier is between zero and 300 yards, day or night.

The 1,000-yard shot is not what we should be practicing for. It is a waste of time for the most part unless you are a purist. We call them "bullet heads." They make their own ammunition to ensure they have the most accurate available; not practical for a military sniper that can fire hundreds of rounds per week and still have time to train for a multitude of other skills in order to do their job. It is always a good idea to start with the most basic skills of shooting, moving, and communicating; they will keep you alive in the worst of situations. Another question I get all the time is, what is the best rifle and caliber? My standard answer is, "The one you practice with." It doesn't matter what the caliber is if you can't hit your target. Remember, most engagements are less than 200 yards.

With technology being what it is today, I believe the days of the classic sniper mission are nearly over, or already gone. Why? With the instant news cycle the way it is currently, the capture or loss of a sniper team in the field would be instant failure for our senior leaders. No matter whether they were successful on their mission or not, the loss would be unacceptable to the public after being blasted out by the media. Technology such as the armed unmanned aerial vehicle, or drone, has made the sniper obsolete. The weapons and optics used by Special Forces today basically can make every operator a sniper. It is time to move on and change strategies from a World War II mindset of holding ground, with soldiers paying the price for holding it, only to give it back when it becomes politically acceptable to do so. How many times have you seen that exact same strategy play itself out in the past 50 years? Senior military leadership has done a disservice to the president (Democrat and Republican) and this country by offering only a "bomb, invade, hold ground, extract" strategy. Politicians need to understand the only way to succeed at war with that particular strategy is to first WIN the war, then understand there will be American troops on the ground for decades like they have been in Germany, Japan, and Korea.

# CHAPTER 19

# Understand the Game before Getting on the Field

Naval Combat Demolition Units and Underwater Demolition Teams were some of the first Special Forces units to integrate during World War II. Native Americans and African Americans fought side by side as early Frogmen. I attribute this to the early creators of the Teams and their focus on standards. It didn't matter who you were as long as you could do the job. That is still the way it is to this day. Standards are the key. Whether it be a haircut, or physical, mental, or behavioral standards, once those standards are set, you have to stick to them. Changing standards for the sake of change is the absolute worst thing you can do to an organization. Standards, however, need to be based in reality.

A candidate must be able to complete a minimum of 11 pull-ups to pass the SEAL physical screening test. Upper body strength is essential for all SEALs in order to complete many of our basic mission sets—climbing a wire caving ladder to board a ship, for example. A typical climb is approximately 40 feet carrying a war load of 60–75 pounds of equipment. Eleven pull-ups are actually nothing like that but the standard for initial training is realistic and can be accomplished by anyone who works at the skill. Water competency is a bit more difficult to measure, but the candidate must know how to swim and be comfortable in the water. BUD/S will teach you how to do it better if you make it past the first step. Race and religion have nothing to do with your success in this case. I can truly say the Teams are colorblind. Do your job and do it well and you will advance.

Women are now allowed to try out for all Special Operations positions in the U.S. military. This is a major change from the past when female support sailors were not allowed at the SEAL Team at all until the late 1980s, let alone actually trying to become a SEAL. Since all SEALs have to accomplish the same job, the standards became even more important while figuring out how to accept women into the ranks. I am sure that one day there will be a woman who makes it through BUD/S training. The real problems begin once she graduates training. I believe it would be a crime to send her to a regular SEAL Team with multitudes of her male counterparts. She will be a one of a kind and should be placed in a special unit of some sort that can utilize her unique skill sets. My question to you is—will it be worth it? In my opinion, it is not. The cost and time involved takes away from the main mission of BUD/S, which is to train SEALs and get them ready for war. Bringing a very few women into the mix takes time and money and is frankly a distraction from the mission. I know this will make some people unhappy, but that is the way I feel. Politics, in theory, should not interfere with common sense.

I was assigned to Naval Recruit Command in Great Lakes, Illinois, as the primary Navy SEAL recruiter/dive motivator for 24 months. It was one of the most difficult positions I have ever filled, and I am glad to have gotten out of there in one piece. My direct boss, and the admiral above her, had never actually commanded a ship, let alone a Navy SEAL. Their experience came through academics and leading at non-warfighting commands such as Great Lakes. My job was to recruit sailors already in the Navy to become SEALs. This idea was a win/win for Naval Special Warfare since the candidates were already in the Navy and all they had to do was pass the screening test to get a chance to go to BUD/S. This process was a lose/lose for the rest of the Navy. If I was able to convince sailors to try out, and if they passed the screening test, they would be eligible for a new set of orders. What that meant was that if the sailor had signed up to work on a ship, he was now on his way to becoming a Navy SEAL. Big Navy, or at least the personnel responsible for manning the Navy, didn't like it one bit but that was the system I was handed. At least Big Navy ended up getting about 70 percent of them back when they quit BUD/S.

I realized very quickly I would not get a lot of support from the Command or leadership. One of the problems I discovered very quickly was the entire base had very few pull-up bars for sailors to practice on. If you can't work out, you can't pass the screening test. I would never be allowed to erect pull-up bars around the base, so I enlisted some friends at the Navy Hull Technician school (welders) to construct portable pull-up bars. We placed the bars into various locations so a sailor could walk by the bars and knock out a few pull-ups and be on his way. Pull-up numbers at the screening test increased dramatically. As the lead dive motivator, my role was also to recruit personnel for all the other Naval Special Warfare programs such as Explosive Ordnance Detection, Navy Diver (Hardhat) and Navy Rescue swimmers. The screening test for each of these trades was less strenuous than the SEAL test. The other specialties also accepted women to try out.

In my two years as lead recruiter for Navy specialty units, I did not see one woman that could pass any of the standards. I would actually come out when a woman was testing to cheer her on because I wanted them to succeed; I wanted at least one to make it to the next level. Unfortunately, none did. The other problem I had was with minority recruiting. The main reason a majority of the candidates did not pass the screening test was that they simply could not swim or swam poorly. I am not going to get into what I believe were the reasons for this, but standards are made for a reason. Sure, we would go the extra mile to help train an individual who was close to passing the test, but bootcamp isn't the place to teach someone how to swim. Recruiting minorities into the SEALs is very important to the overall strength of the unit. I was supposed to help grow those numbers so we could be more effective at our mission. I tried my best and, fortunately, was able to pass a few into the community.

About a year after arriving in Great Lakes, I was ready to go. The Navy didn't agree, however, and I had 12 more months of pain to go. During that time, I was visited by the admiral in charge of all the SEALs; he was based in Coronado, California. He tasked me to locate a building on base which would be suitable to start a program to prepare future trainees for the rigors of BUD/S before they were shipped to California. The theory was Pre–BUD/S would create more SEALs because they would better understand what they were getting into. What it actually created was a better-qualified class of quitters. The attrition rate of over 70 percent hasn't changed at all and the Navy was spending a bunch of time and money to babysit these guys in Illinois before they shipped out to California. I did what I was asked and started looking for a suitable building on base to run the course. About a week into my search, I got a phone call from the aide of the admiral in charge at Great Lakes to come to her office for a visit. Really? Maybe she wanted to check in on me and review SEAL recruiting. Regardless, I put on a proper uniform and traveled to her office expecting a warm welcome.

That is not what I got. The admiral's aide ushered me into the office in front of her desk where she was working. I stood there for a minute looking stupid until she lifted her head and yelled "stand at attention!" Well, this wasn't going well. It turns out my admiral, the one in charge of the SEALs, didn't discuss his plans to open a Pre–BUD/S course on her base. As I went about my merry way looking for proper facilities for the mission, word got back to her what I was doing. Since I technically worked for her, it appeared I was going behind her back, a rogue warrior for lack of a better term. Needless to say, I continued to stand there at attention and receive my tongue lashing until she was sufficiently tired of yelling. I think the only two words out of my mouth at the time were "Yes, ma'am" when she asked if I understood her anger. You can do one of two things at this point. Suck it up and move on or try to explain the situation and how I was put into that situation by my own admiral. I choose to suck it up for a number of reasons: 1. It is less than honorable to throw anyone else under the bus; 2. No one was dying; 3. For all I knew, she already understood what was going on and wanted to prove a point. Who knows?

I walked out with my tail between my legs and learned a very valuable lesson. Make sure you understand the game before getting on the field. Politics seems to change people for the worse. In this case, both my bosses were willing to screw with me for something I did not understand at the time. Now, granted, I have done plenty that has deserved a reprimand, but not in this case. Life went on. We started the new Pre-BUD/S course on schedule. By the end of my tour at Great Lakes, I had made many friends and even tried to help with Big Navy recruiting by bringing in the Navy Parachute Team "Leap Frogs" to do a demonstration for the base (perhaps even get a jump in myself).

# CHAPTER 20

# Trust Your Gut

Parachute operations are one of the highest-risk evolutions any military unit can undertake. There are always at least 100 things that can go wrong at any given time that you have absolutely no control over. Jumping at night makes it even more dangerous, but that is when SEALs typically operate. With over two thousand five hundred jumps under my belt, I have been fortunate to record only two mishaps which could have easily taken my life. Sometimes it is good to be lucky, blessed, or both.

As you become more proficient at parachuting, like any other skill set in the SEALs, you are usually assigned more responsibility managing the training evolution. In my case, I became qualified as a Military Freefall Jumpmaster and Accelerated Freefall Instructor, both of which meant being responsible for the safety of multiple jumpers. I no longer had the luxury of being responsible for just my own actions, but everyone involved in the training.

One of the biggest mistakes involving jumping in my career was during my tenure as the lead training chief at SEAL Team SIX. Many of the newer guys that showed up did not have the necessary skills or qualifications to be assigned to an assault team without advanced parachute training, among other things. Because of the nature of jumping and the risk involved, this form of training took longer than others. The culmination of the course was a full-team, full-equipment jump into an unknown drop zone (DZ)—in this case, somewhere on the U.S. Army base in Fort Campbell, Kentucky. The aircraft was a U.S. Air Force Special Operations C-130. The crew was not happy about the mission because jump operations for them were boring. Too bad. My goal as jumpmaster and lead of the evolution was to have the 30 men exit the aircraft at twilight, so they could see each other when opening, and land at dark. Timing was critical. I had a set time to pull this off.

The aircraft commander on the other hand had a different idea and wanted to get some low-level flight training in before the jump—no problem if he is ready to go at the agreed upon time. First mistake, I should have known better. That plane and crew were there for us, not the other way around. As time passed and we missed our deadline, I became more and more agitated and let my emotions get the best of me. I re-briefed the jumpers in flight to let them know this was going to be a night jump with release control given to the aircraft navigation system. What I should have done in retrospect was to cancel the jump and land the aircraft; but I did not.

We released all 30 new SEALs over the designated drop zone when the green jump light came on at the back ramp of the plane. Or that is what I thought. As it turned out, we were nowhere near the DZ and just released the Team all over the base. Luckily for me, no one was injured. All jumpers and parachutes were recovered and the Team continued on with their mission, glad to be alive, with a little less faith in me. That is a big deal in the SEAL Teams. Landing the aircraft would have been the smartest and safest thing to do, but I was afraid to lose face. How could Navy SEALs not want to conduct a mission just because it got dark out? My own pride clouded my judgement and it could have gotten someone hurt or worse. Every time I have made a mistake during parachute operations, it has been because I didn't trust my training and, more importantly, my gut. Unless someone's life is on the line, stop what you are doing, regroup, and make sure you are making the right decisions. It works every time whether you are getting ready to send a questionable email or text or getting ready to get into an altercation. Stop and think about what you are doing and the outcome.

Slowing down even for a split second can really be the difference between success and failure. Many years later, I ran into a number of the guys on that particular jump. Instead of the expected harassment I deserved, they actually told me the jump was one of the best in their careers. It seems all the things I had preached in training were put to the test on that jump—truly an unknown DZ, in the dark, and everyone had to land safely and find their teammates. Typical training jump operations revolve around safety which eliminates all the realism. Go figure.

# CHAPTER 21

# Never Say Never

I retired from active duty at ST-6 after 22 years as a Master Chief Petty Officer in August of 2000. I had been an assaulter, breacher, lead diver, lead jumper, special projects member, sniper, sniper team leader and sniper squadron leader. The deployments were starting to get to the family and me at this point and the only mission in town was searching for persons indicted for war crimes in Bosnia. I considered myself to have "been there, done that" already. It was not time to hang up my fins however, so I took a job as a civilian employee in the operations department at ST-6. No more deployments for me. At the time there were only a handful of former SEALs hired back to assist in running the team and none of them worked in the operations department, which is the center of any Command. Bottom line: operations is given guidance from the Commanding Officer and is then given the authority to carry out his orders. I did not have any problems giving directions after being on the Team for so long. I believed I would be a good fit. I had many SEAL, civilian and support personnel friends throughout the Command. I knew how to get things done and how to deal with people. I was still part of the team but not the guy kicking down doors. It was a senior leadership position. No written guidance, no rules, trust your gut. I worked directly for the operations officer, a senior Navy SEAL progressing up the officer ranks as part of his career path. Usually, a two-year assignment like all officer positions in the Navy. It was my job to provide continuity and give guidance as a long-term Team member. It was a good job for a short time until the unthinkable happened. 9/11. When the attacks on our country occurred on 9/11 it changed my life as it did for countless others. ST-6 was at the forefront of any retaliation strike that our leaders were going to hand to our enemies and I wanted in. Having only been off active duty for a year, it was easy to make a few phone calls to get me back. Events were moving quickly at home and with the team. Explanations were given, decisions were being made, and I was a few weeks away from returning to active roles. That is when my boss, the operations officer, asked me to reconsider the change. What I did not understand was that the entire Command was about to deploy, leaving a huge leadership void. The operations officer was about to leave for an undetermined amount of time and was asking me to stay and hold down the fort. Decision time. On the one hand, I could stay where I was and help arguably the greatest fighting force on the planet. On the other, I could rejoin and be assigned to any SEAL Team that needed a Master Chief. In the end, I believed I could make more of a difference in operations and remained there for the next 12 years, including multiple deployments to wonderful places like Afghanistan. Never say never.

CHAPTER 22

# Don't Judge a SEAL by His Cover

I watched the Twin Towers come down as did most people in this country—on TV. What I understood however was that we were going to war. No one at that time could have understood the length or depth of what was coming. But we were doing what we were trained for. Once I made the decision to remain in operations, I settled in for the ride. Myself and another fellow Master Chief basically ran the department for the foreseeable future. Leadership tried to keep up by assigning various operations officers to oversee us but due to the war, these guys were more valuable forward in Afghanistan and eventually Iraq than they were at home. I started to keep a list of the many "O's" who took the job but stopped after 25–30 in a matter of five years. One guy lasted only three days before new orders sent him away. Another day in the life of Ops. My time was not without controversy. I had many run-ins with other officers who could not accept the fact that a former Master Chief was now giving them orders. Of course, I was only following my own orders, but that did not make any difference. Early on in Ops, I was given a Navy SEAL reservist as an Ops O. "Sacrilege." What in the world did a damn reservist know about running ST-6? I can tell you. Little or nothing. Or so I thought. He turned out to be one of my better bosses during my time in Ops. Go figure, wrong again. He was also responsible for single-handedly keeping me from getting fired by the Commanding Officer. I had ruffled quite a few feathers doing my job and several of the officers throughout the Command were not happy. They complained to the CO, at which point he considered giving me the boot. The reservist had been there long enough to see what I did on a daily basis and convinced the CO that it would be a mistake to get rid of me. I was not told of the incident until months later when the reservist had moved on and was deploying in leadership roles for the Team. He waited to tell me the story because he knew I would have confronted the CO about questioning my abilities. Probably would not have ended well for me and he knew it. That CO moved on and the next and the next, while I remained. The reservist ended up with more time deployed overseas than any other Navy SEAL. He also retired as an admiral.

# CHAPTER 23

# Think before Hitting Send

I have a daughter who is a Millennial and a son who is a Gen Z. I have been forced, along with all others in the older generations, to adapt to changes in technology and communications. It was probably easier for me than most because, as a Navy SEAL, our goal was always to innovate and find the next best piece of equipment or technique. I realize the importance of social media but am not particularly impressed with where it has led us as a society. I believe young people are losing the skill to communicate in person, face to face. They depend on a smart phone of some sort and a keypad. Fire and forget, much like the modern-day military drone pilot that sees things on a video screen; it is far easier to detach from a Hellfire strike if you are not even in the same country as the person you are shooting at.

Maybe one day there will be no use for Special Forces. Wars will be decided by some method we cannot even contemplate at this time. In the meantime, however, new tech, such as the ever-changing social media platforms, is bad for any type of personal or operational security. It is far too easy for an enemy to monitor an individual's Facebook or Snapchat feed looking for information. Pictures from deployments find their way to the internet where they can be studied and identified. Deployment and re-deployment dates are readily exchanged between family and friends in totally innocent ways, but this gives others information that can lead to disaster. My point? Some of our foreign counterparts require their Special Forces members to agree "not" to use any form of social media while on active duty. I see no downside to this of course, having come up long before there were computers, let alone cell phones. There are many different ways to communicate that are more secure than social media. This is not only important to the military, but to any business with intellectual property worth stealing.

One of the funniest pranks I have pulled in my long history of pranks was directly related to technology. My daughter, who was 15 at the time, had a slumber party with about ten other girls at our home. Each one of them had their own cell phone and proceeded to either talk on the phone, take pictures, or send text messages at the party. What was the sense of bringing everyone over if no one was going to talk to each other? I just so happened to have a portable cell-phone jammer in my car which I immediately grabbed, and decided to conduct a social experiment.

I plopped down in my chair to watch TV, which happened to be fairly close to where all the girls were congregating on their phones. I slowly reached into my pocket and turned on the device. Within 30 seconds, all 11 girls were clamoring about not having signal. I helpfully suggested they go outside on the driveway to see if the signal would improve. They followed me like lemmings. Of course, the signal did not improve because the jammer was still on in my pocket. They were becoming visibly shaken. I turned the jammer off. Their signal came back full force and everyone shouted in glee. Thirty seconds later, I walked toward the front door and turned the jammer on again, shutting down the latest round of texts, pictures, and conversations. It was glorious. Some of the girls were jumping up and down in anger. How could their trusty cell phones all go out at the same time? I suggested the backyard, with deep concern on my face. The lemmings followed and were rewarded with one minute of service only to be shut down once again. Life was cruel, but I was worse.

We continued on this path for approximately 45 minutes until they finally decided to go back in the house, play a game, and talk. Mission accomplished. After some snacks, games, and conversation, the girls were now bored; the phones came back out only to be shut down once again. Helpful as ever, I suggested they try going outside one more time, but I would not accompany them. It seems the jammer had enough strength and range to work from inside the home on the second floor. Time for a cocktail so I could watch the fun from the window. As I sat on the windowsill observing the girls' behavior, my daughter had the foresight to realize I was up to something. Why would I be watching from the window? Surely, I had a show to watch or something. Then it hit her.

I saw the angry look in her eye as she screamed "Dad!" and raced up the steps to confront me. By that time, I was laughing so hard I immediately spilled the beans and showed her the jammer. I was lucky to escape the wrath of the teenage hit squad and promised to turn off the jammer for the night. The story spread like wildfire and unfortunately the jammer never worked as effectively as it had the very first time until I took it to my favorite watering hole—a whole new set of victims ripe for the picking. I hope the girls finally realized somewhere way back in their minds that maybe, just maybe, they were a bit more dependent on technology than they should have been. We will see.

It was an email that taught me the rule of never writing something down that you are not willing to share with the world. A lesson learnt the hard way. In the early days of the War on Terror—I'm talking the month after 9/11—SEAL Team SIX (ST-6) was in Afghanistan. One of my sniper buddies from my days in Somalia was deployed while I was working operations Stateside.

One day, I was sitting in my office and received an email from my friend asking what I thought about a junior officer who had recently also been deployed but had only been at the team for a few years. I thought about the question because I wanted to give my friend an accurate answer which would help him deal with the individual overseas. At the time, I was not a fan of the individual but didn't want to let my personal feelings get in the way. I wrote, "Watch your back." Fairly short but clear. I wasn't sure the individual could be trusted in all situations. He was younger and less experienced than my Master Chief teammate.

No sooner than I had pressed send did the secure phone on my desk ring. It was, you guessed it, the individual I was talking about. It seems the group was sharing one email address due to lack of resources in Afghanistan, a little fact my friend had failed to share.

The conversation was not pleasant. After all, he was an officer and one thing I always try to uphold is military order and discipline. I ended up doing the moonwalk backwards and apologizing, mainly because I never should have sent the email and, secondly, I didn't want it to come back on my friend. I had to eat some major crow that day and for years to come.

The individual would move on to become the Commanding Officer of ST-6 and later an admiral. We had a good working relationship. I followed orders, but I am sure he doesn't trust me, similar to the same way I feel about him. As it turns out, this same officer was actually in command at ST-6 when I decided to depart the Team after over twenty-five years. I have to thank him for that; he made the decision easy. I did not like the direction he was taking the Team in and it was better for me to leave than stay and bitch about it. As it turns out, leaving was the right call at that time.

I learned a valuable lesson that day. Think before you speak, email, or text.

CHAPTER 24

# Listen to Your People

Each Command in the U.S. Navy conducts what is called a Command Climate Survey intended to measure the morale of troops from most junior to most senior. It isn't perfect, but it is anonymous, meaning personnel have a tendency to open up more and answer the questions honestly. A SEAL Team is unlike regular U.S. Navy Commands. Everything and everyone is driven by the mission. Personnel that don't recognize that are either transferred or marginalized quickly. You can imagine all the different issues and problems dealt with on a daily basis at a place such as SEAL Team SIX (ST-6).

The two issues that came up every time during the Command Climate Survey, believe it or not, were the disparity of treatment between the SEALs and support personnel, and parking. Out of all the issues in the world today, those were the two that continued to be brought up year after year. At first, I ignored the complaints but, after time, I knew neither problem was going to go away so maybe we should spend some time trying to address the concern.

There are seven support personnel for every SEAL. SEALs are amazing individuals and can do almost superhuman tasks, but we can do very little by ourselves. We need medics, Seabees, communicators, intelligence, admin, operations, facilities, travel, comptroller, weapons and ammunition support to name a few. Without everyone working together for the same goal, the mission would certainly fail. Paying attention to the word on the street is critical. Morale is a tough item to gauge across a large organization, so it you have the chance to make a difference, do it.

Navy SEALs are arguably some of the best athletes in the world. We work out for two to three hours every day besides our normal training schedule. SEALs, however, will not walk an extra 20 feet in the parking lot in order to park legally. Maybe it is human nature. I know most of the guys aren't lazy, they just want to park closest to the locker room. In the big picture, parking was not a life-or-death problem. It could, however, slow down or stop someone from dealing with a life-or-death situation. Unchecked, personnel would block major choke points which would stop the movement of critical equipment or people. When you are on a timeline, every second counts. Then there's medical support. Accidents happen all the time at a SEAL team, everything from gunshot wounds to heart attacks. Blocking the ambulance from getting to the scene is unacceptable.

The other item from the survey was the opinion the SEALs were treated differently to support personnel. True. No way to avoid that one. The SEALs are doing the fighting and the dying for the most part, with a few exceptions. They are the ones risking their lives on a daily basis and suffering the never-ending series of injuries that go with the lifestyle. Of course, SEALs can't do the mission alone. Never could. The smart SEALs know how to work with their teammates and not alienate them. The stupid SEALs think, somehow, they are better than everyone else and expect everything to be handed to them on a silver platter. I didn't have much time for those SEALs. They didn't get it.

As I started working the parking problem at the Command, I realized most of the problems came from the SEALs that didn't get it. Ninety-five percent of the Command followed the rules, parked correctly, and were good sailors. It was the 5 percent I had to deal with. If I could figure out a way to punish them, it would take care of most of the parking problem and make it look to our support personnel that someone cared about them. They understood all along who the culprits were for illegal parking and many of the other problems suffered at the Command.

Every vehicle at the time was required to have a base sticker on the front bumper or windshield which would give them access to the base each morning. A base security guard would check to see if you had a sticker and then wave you in if you did. No sticker meant no entry and a trip to the base security office for a new one, which was a real pain. It took up to several hours to get a new sticker if you had all the paperwork to include registration and proof of insurance. No one liked to go for a new sticker.

My plan was that I would find the violators, scrape their stickers, and let them deal with base security. A typical violator wouldn't even know they were "scraped" until the next morning when trying to get on base. Once the base police turned them around, they knew exactly what had just happened. I never feared for my life, but I did keep my head on a swivel. It wouldn't be uncommon for my car or locker to be a target of retaliation. The scraping had its desired effect. People started parking better. Talk around the Command proved the 95 percent that followed the rules were appreciative of what I was doing. It actually took very little time. Usually when I took a trip outside the office to go work out or attend a meeting, I would make a mental note of the offending vehicles; if they were in place when I returned, they were scraped.

Some violators were so over the top that they required special treatment. I couldn't be everywhere all the time, so I had help, usually from my Seabee (Construction Battalion) friends who could not move a big piece of equipment due to illegal parking. They would give me a call, report the violator, and ask what I wanted to do. If the vehicle was blocking an intersection, it was towed immediately and the offender had to visit me in person to explain. If they were in someone else's parking spot, such as the Commanding Officer's, they were booted. A "boot" is a wonderful device that locks on to the wheel of the vehicle so it cannot move. Again, the person would have to visit me in person to explain their actions. This step was dependent on my schedule which could also take some time out of their day. Because this was a SEAL Team, there were many ways to handle problems such as a boot that did not require a face-to-face meeting. One individual actually went to the breacher shop and borrowed a quicky saw to cut the boot off. Breachers are the specialists that gain entry into any locked space whether it be a building, car, ship, plane, or anything else we needed to get into. This guy was a five percenter through and through and had apparently had multiple other issues within his team and was shit-canned (relieved) immediately. I always felt a bit bad for that one. Not really.

Personnel were parking correctly and one of the perceived disparities between SEALs and support was being addressed. I enjoyed the task, but I had to be careful. Well-trained guys half my age do not take kindly to being scraped, towed, or booted. The last thing I wanted was a physical altercation in the parking lot. Lose-lose for everyone. Sniping was not an option for this mission, so I had to use my stealth abilities to find the violator's car and scrape the stickers before anyone was the wiser. I could cleanly walk past a bumper and scrape the sticker in seconds and be on my way. The target site was always the most dangerous whether it be in combat or fighting parking violators. The plan succeeded, there was peace in the parking world once again. I had to draw the line when the Seabees offered to train me how to drive a tow truck. Maybe I like the excitement. I believe it was similar to being a repo man—risk and reward.

Unfortunately, not everyone enjoyed my tactics, and the CO and executive officer were getting complaints about my heavy-handed methods; they were actually contemplating letting me go. Fortunately, my officer counterpart and I had a great working relationship and became friends. As the headshed (what we called the leadership) was about to shit-can me, my boss at the time put in a good word for me and ended the situation.

What I did not realize at the time is that many leaders are not willing to make the hard call when it comes to the possibility of angering the masses—in this case the SEAL Team. I, on the other hand, was not in charge so I had no qualms about acting as the "adult" in many situations and actually saying "No" to people or holding them accountable for their actions. I think, in the long run, the headshed realized it was better to let me hold the line than for them to do it. That way they could stay above the fray and always have a way out, should it come to it. I didn't have a problem with my role in the scheme of maneuver, in fact I relished it because I knew there were very few individuals that could or would actually take the part. I had plenty of friends and was not there to make any more. My mission, like it had always been, was to get the job done in the best, most efficient way possible. Period.

Another issue, which could sometimes be worse than the parking, was cage allocation. Each SEAL was assigned a 10 × 10 × 10-foot cage to store all their equipment. It literally looks like a cage in the zoo—a wire mesh cube with a rolling wire mesh door that you can secure. We had to be ready to go to war in a matter of hours, so all the gear had to be packed in bags, labeled, and weighed at all times. The cages were a way to store your equipment exactly the way you wanted and gave you a little bit of property you had total control over on the compound. Cages were a very personal item so, as you can imagine, there was always drama involved. There were clear and concise lines or borders between the various elements. You could visit the other section, but there was no way you could move into an empty cage in another group's area. Rules were rules and everyone was happy to help with this problem. Of course, we couldn't leave a cage vacant if someone needed a space, so it become a negotiation every time.

Property matters usually fell on the Command Master Chief to handle. All were my friends, so it was not hard to contact them to try to work the deal. The problem was two-thirds of the Command was usually traveling at any given time so making quick decisions with consensus was difficult to say the least. The most difficult trades usually involved a cage move which no one wanted. Hours of lugging bags, guns, and personal gear appealed to no one. Life is not fair, especially to the new guys or junior guys. Many were forced to move to create peace. Inside deals were the norm. What ended up happening was that most of the senior guys ended up in the center of their little kingdoms with junior guys on the periphery. That way, the decision makers wouldn't be put in a position to have to move for the greater good. It always fascinated me what guys thought was important—like parking. Of course, I always had a good cage in a strategic area along with a pristine parking spot. After all, someone has to make the decisions.

The Second Amendment is alive and well in our country because of men and women like the ones I worked with every day at the team. However, that didn't mean we had the same rights that every American enjoys outside our compound. We had every weapon imaginable at ST-6 and for good reason. We were required to be proficient with all of them in order to do our job. At one time, the allocation of 9-mm ammunition at ST-6 was greater than the entire United States Marine Corps. We shot a lot and were very good. Man for man, we could have competed with any other military unit in the world. With that fact in mind, we were not allowed to carry firearms on base. No concealed carry and no carry inside a vehicle brought on base. Some of the most highly trained personnel in the world were supposed to be protected by contract guards and U.S. Navy personnel between assignments. Even the professional Navy Police or Master of Arms had very limited training. To top it off, certain U.S. Navy civilian employees that worked at the Command actually complained about guys carrying weapons into their workspace to conduct business. There were many times each day when administrative tasks had to be accomplished. Since we were training most of the time, that meant carrying weapons. The threat of lawsuits by civilian employees that felt threatened eventually ended the practice of carrying guns outside the designated live-fire ranges, or to and from those ranges. Weapons are strictly accountable in all military units. Going to the armory to lock up your weapon takes time we didn't have. The process of getting in the secure storage, which was there for a good reason, also took away the valuable time needed to make a phone call or get a new ID card. Cell phones are a big no-no inside a secure compound, at least for the guys that followed the rules.

Similar to the no weapons rules, we had to deal with Rules of Engagement (ROE) on a daily basis. We can all say we love lawyers, right? Well, at ST-6, you couldn't do anything without a legal review. Most of the lawyers, otherwise known as "Jags" (Judge Advocate General, Navy lawyers), were good to go, but not all. The best advice I have ever been taught, whether you are a lawyer or not, is "Never tell the boss 'No.' Tell him how he can accomplish the mission within the rules." It may not be the exact way he asked for, but at least you offered him an alternative solution before he makes a final decision anyway. In the long run, it wasn't hard to get the boss what he wanted since the Jags were the ones responsible for writing the ROEs in the first place. It was their job to keep us out of trouble even though at times it seemed like they were interfering with our mission. The lawyers that automatically gave a "No" answer were marginalized and pushed aside. Find the person that would give you the conditional "Yes." The most successful SEALs at ST-6 understood that. Never settle for a no, find the yes. Some even created the yes in their own minds. Risky move, but where there is no clear guidance, we will create it. The biggest risk to any of our missions was being distracted by bullshit.

CHAPTER 25

# Make a Plan

Change is hard. After 34 years working for the U.S. Navy as an active-duty SEAL and in civilian service since I was 17, leaving was a scary thought. In the Teams, we call it quitting. It doesn't matter how long you have been doing a job, once you decide to leave, you are a quitter. All in good fun of course, but, as far as others are concerned, once the decision is made you are excluded from any decision-making process and politely shown the door. Of course, you get a going away party with some plaques and other knick-knacks, but that is about it. No big deal. I did the same thing countless times to friends who had made the same decisions. The weird part about this story is that you never knew for sure what was going to happen. I have seen people years later at the Team thinking they had moved on only to find they had been there the whole time. Military life, especially in the Teams, is very transient. The only absolute is retirement.

Even retirement has a gray area if you decide to move from active duty to civilian service (basically doing the same job you used to do without the guns). I deployed around the world as a civilian member of SEAL Team SIX (ST-6) for many years. Everyone was needed during the Global War on Terror; it didn't matter if you were a civilian or not. It was common to be sent to places like Afghanistan and Iraq. The young guys did the fighting. The old guys did the coordination. Still in the fight but not quite.

What else can you do after years on the front line. Quit cold turkey? Some could do it; I couldn't. It was the highest honor to be part of the team, regardless of your actual position. Unfortunately, SEALs find themselves pigeonholed into certain career fields once the decision is made to move on—security, shooting instructor, contractor, physical fitness, or government civilian, to name a few career fields which are most common among former SEALs. Of course, there are exceptions, usually officers with a background in finance or something similar that can move on to a big company with the SEAL "brand" helping them in the front door.

An issue that baffles me to this day is the fact many of my brothers fail to plan for the day they are forced to move on. Whether it be their choice or not, many will not accept the inevitable and actually have a plan. There is a saying in the military that any good plan does not survive the first contact with the enemy. In this case, the enemy is retirement. Many of my teammates know the end is coming but fail to come up with a game plan. Planning is the bread and butter of the military, yet they fail to take care of themselves. I understand the problem since I went through the transition from military to civilian myself. I made jokes about it. I had a plan. I was going to be the Executive Director of the Navy SEAL Museum. Couldn't quite cut away all together from the Teams. The job was familiar and not that far of a stretch in my mind. Clueless once again. Hadn't I thought the same thing when I wanted to join the SEAL Teams back in the beginning? What did I know about running a museum? I knew how to be a SEAL, lead people, and make decisions. Hopefully that would be a good place to start. The first thing I had to do was learn about the past. I had to make myself a subject matter expert about everything SEAL-related, or at least be knowledgeable about each. Clueless. I am still learning something new each day. I will say, however, there are only a few dozen former SEALs that have more knowledge than my team at the Museum.

# CHAPTER 26

# Learn from Mistakes and Grow

The National Navy SEAL Museum was dedicated in 1985 in Fort Pierce, Florida, to much fanfare in the Naval Special Warfare community. A sleepy little museum, it took the home of the Florida State Treasure Museum. Along comes a Frogman with an idea in 1984 and thus, after much work with the county, the "UDT SEAL Museum" was born.

Barely surviving, the museum catered to the military buff and the Veterans Day celebration we called the "Muster" (a Naval term for a gathering at the fantail of a ship to receive the orders of the day). Many an old Frogman gathered at the museum for that three-day weekend. All that changed, however, with the killing of America's most wanted terrorist by my SEAL friends in 2011. Life probably would have gone on as normal had it not been for then Vice President Joe Biden and his outing of SEAL Team SIX (ST-6) to the media; he had officially exposed the unit who had taken bin Laden out, putting the SEALs, their families, and the community at risk for reprisals. If it had been you or me, I can assure you we would have spent some time behind bars, but that is not the way the world works. As the Navy SEALs began to gain notoriety, so did the Navy SEAL Museum. Attendance grew, donations grew, and the museum was on its way up ever so slowly.

Enter stage right. I moved to Florida after 34 years of government service, burned out, and ready for a change. Not knowing a thing about museums, but much about Navy SEALs, I figured it couldn't be that hard; I could learn, and I did. I put myself out there at every Rotary Club luncheon or men's club dinner I was invited to. Slowly I started to figure it out. My goal? To build a world-class military museum preserving the history of the Navy SEALs and our predecessors, honor our fallen at the Navy SEAL Memorial, and support our families through a program we now call the Trident House Charities Program. I built a team of like-minded individuals and brought in another Master Chief I had worked with for over twenty years to help me run the joint. We raised money, we worked hard, we played hard.

Before leaving the military, I had never held a position for longer than three years. That is the way the military works. Everything changes on a regular basis according to schedule. Commanding Officers come and go every two years along with all the enlisted senior staff. That is the way of the world in the Teams. Some changes are good; some are bad depending on leadership. As you spend more time in the Teams, in theory, you should move up in responsibility. Age is not necessarily a bad thing in the Teams. You may lose a step or two, but you have gained that much more experience. Kicking doors and clearing rooms is a young SEAL's job. The more seasoned SEALs remain outside the building directing multiple attacks and coordinating among the Team and outside support. Successfully completing the mission is the only thing that matters, not what your role in that mission happened to be on that particular day.

Leading as a civilian in many respects is much different than leading while on active duty. Dealing with civilians/non-military personnel was a challenge at first. I was used to giving and following orders with very little questioning. Not quite the case in the real world. I had to account for things like other people's feelings. As Executive Director (ED), and now Chief Executive Officer (CEO) of the National Navy SEAL Museum, I also found myself in the position of counsellor and mentor, which was okay since I had been doing that for many years. The principles of leadership, however, remained the same. It was the execution that changed drastically. I could no longer take it for granted that personnel would listen and follow directions. I had to become kinder and gentler until I had time to understand my new teammates. Once they got to know me, and I them, all that "kinder, gentler" went out the door. If you are not doing your job, I will let you know. No crying at work. The key is respect. I respect my co-workers for what they do, period. If someone is failing, I try to help and provide any guidance which may help. No one is perfect, least of all me.

I think the hardest concept for my new teammates to accept was that I trusted them to do their jobs without micromanaging them. This was the only way I knew how to run things. I was forming a new SEAL Team, not one that carried guns or blew things up, but one that had a mission we were going to accomplish. If they were looking for direction, I would certainly give it, so be aware of what you are actually asking for.

As a military man, I am used to taking orders. The chain of command was engrained in my soul after many years of duty. To this day I still address officers by their rank or "sir," mostly as a sign of respect. What I wasn't prepared for was answering to a board of directors. Not one or two people, but sometimes up to 15 members voting on your fate. I don't want to say I was a political novice since I knew very well how to play the political game in order to achieve the mission. This was on a whole new level. Everything had to be run by the book in order to keep everyone clean in case of scrutiny. One of the things I had been taught about decision making was, first, always try to do the right thing; second, would you be willing to stand in front of a camera to explain exactly what your decision-making process was? I had no problems with either of these factors. What I didn't realize was the effort needed to build consensus and bullet-proof majorities when it came time to vote on initiatives I wanted to carry out. It was easy in the military. The boss or Commanding Officer made all the major decisions. If he said "no," I would carry on and not think a thing about the subject again. A board of directors is a whole different animal. Yes, decisions are possible, even after an initial no.

Proper, prior planning prevents piss poor performance. The 7Ps. Great words to live by but very hard to keep up. Like all good organizations, most people serve to further the mission. Some, however, have their own agendas and must be called out or marginalized as soon as possible. The other realization I had was that I needed to be willing to resign or be fired at a moment's notice. It is more of a mindset thing. If you ever become too dependent on anything such as a job, you will never be happy. Worrying about making mistakes tends to eat you alive and make you an ineffective leader and decision maker. Make your mistakes, learn by them, and try not to repeat them. That is why history and heritage are so important to everyone. Without documentation from the past, you are destined to make the same mistakes over and over again. We had a saying at ST-6, "If you don't like a decision, wait a few years and the decision will be changed back." Full-circle logic in most cases because leaders did not realize many of the decisions they thought were new were actually already tried and scrubbed for whatever reason. Times change, technology changes even faster; change for the sake of change is bad for everyone.

# CHAPTER 27

# It Never Hurts to Have Another Set of Eyes

I have made more than two thousand five hundred parachute jumps in my career, with three or four bad landings. Unfortunately, it is the landings that get you in the end. The first I recall was during parachute training in Arizona. A typical trip was 7 to 10 days in which we would accomplish 30–50 jumps, many with full equipment at night. By the end of one trip, we had accomplished all our goals and decided to have a competition jump where we would see who could land closest to the X marked on the ground. SEALs tend to be very competitive and I have since learned jump competitions are probably not the safest events to end a trip with. Sort of like the last ski run of the day when everyone gets hurt. The exit from the aircraft was uneventful but, nonetheless, I was always fully aware this could potentially turn bad at any moment. The term for deploying your parachute in the military is "opening shock" for good reason; sometimes it was nice and smooth, other times it felt like the heels of your feet hit the back of your head. I was laser focused when the canopy inflated to get myself in the best position with the wind to win the competition. As I concentrated on the drop zone (DZ) and target, I lost my grip on common sense. The competition meant nothing but bragging rights but still I tried to win. Just before landing, the smart parachutist flares their canopy which slows down the 'chute and changes the angle of descent, producing a nice stand-up landing. I, however, was so focused I tried to will myself to the X and ended up hitting the ground full speed with no flare, only to land 10 feet away from the target.

If I had flared my canopy, I would have had a soft landing on the X. Lesson learned—no competition is worth a black and blue body.

The second near fatality I encountered while jumping happened during a demonstration jump. Again, I was intent on making a precision jump in a narrow drop zone which I could have easily changed 50 yards east for a nice golf course. Unfortunately, there were numerous palm trees surrounding the target, not to mention a large crowd of senior golfers, but that did not deter me. As I came in, I tried to shoot between two large palm trees which would have worked out perfectly had it not been for a gust of wind which pushed me into one of the trees. I hit about 20 feet up, my canopy collapsed and I crashed to the ground, fracturing my right leg and pelvis. Humiliation at its finest. I was carted off to the hospital for what would become a six-month recovery period involving crutches, walkers, and a cane before I could start jumping again (really).

The third and final near-death jumping experience involved a whole series of screw ups for which I can blame only myself. In 2016, Barbara and I planned to renew our vows in Wisconsin in front of my friends and family, since they could not make it to the actual wedding in Vero Beach, Florida. My sister, who lives on a beautiful lake right outside of Milwaukee, Wisconsin, offered the location and set up. I thought it would be a great idea to parachute into the wedding. Why not? I had fully healed from the palm tree incident and was ready to go.

There were so many things wrong with this scenario from the beginning, I often wonder how I survived the SEAL Teams. The DZ was small and on the side of a lake. It was surrounded by trees and homes. I had never jumped there before and I had no experienced ground crew. What could go wrong? My back-up plan was to land in the lake should I not be able to make the wedding DZ. Unfortunately, my back-up plan was filled with boaters who had come to see the Navy SEAL jump into his wedding, which severely cut down the available area for plan B. I had wind streamers on the DZ which would let me know which direction the wind was going during landing, which is critical for success. As I found out later, the wind changed direction as I exited the aircraft. I made my way to the earth to the loving arms of my wife, mother, and father, who had never watched me jump before. Again, laser focus on the DZ caused me to realize too late I was not going to make it. Plan B was in action but about 200 feet below where I should have made the decision. As I maneuvered my way to the water, I saw a pier jutting out that I was sure I would fly over and safely land right next to. My right foot caught the edge of the pier at 25 miles per hour, causing me to stop immediately and literally ripping my foot off.

On a funny note, before the paramedics shut the doors of the ambulance, my wife ran up and asked me to sit up so she could put my wedding ring on my finger and say "I do." I did as I was asked, morphine and all, and she slipped the ring on my finger and said it. The paramedics were not amused and believed my wife was trying to marry me while under the influence of drugs. Later on, in the hospital, they listed my wife as my fiancée until she could get it straightened out.

My right ankle was pulverized. My foot was actually torn off my leg at the ankle with only a flap of skin, one tendon, and one artery holding it on. Surprisingly there was not a lot of blood. I remember pulling myself out of the water, looking at my foot, or what was left of it, and yelling for someone to call 911. I tried not to look at it again because I didn't want to put myself in shock. I couldn't feel anything for the first 20 minutes while I waited to be transported to the hospital. Around the 20-minute mark, it started to hurt. There is a wonderful drug called morphine that was created for just this occasion. The paramedics were more than obliging and the pain went away. The next thing I remember, besides the "proposal," was waking up in the Emergency Room (ER) and yelling at whomever was pulling on my foot to let go. The doctors thought I was sufficiently anesthetized for the repositioning of my foot in its proper position. I was not, and continued to yell until they gave me enough drugs to knock me out.

Luckily, my brother and wife were both in the ER looking after me during the time I was out. I'm not going to judge their decision making in times of stress, but I do want to ask the question, what would you do? On a scale of 1 to 10, one being the best case and 10 being the worst for the condition of my ankle and the prospect of a below-the-knee amputation (yes, amputation), the doctor actually gave me a seven. To my SEAL mind, a seven meant cut it off, but I wasn't awake. They were in an impossible situation but that doesn't mean I can't bring up the story every now and then and ask what others would do when given the same criteria. It is fun to watch my brother squirm in these situations and finally tell me to @$%& off. I am much more cautious with my wife on this subject. I may be slow and accident prone, but I am not stupid.

They decided to try to keep the foot and put Humpty Dumpty back together again. It was amazing the doctor could do it at all. There were so many pins and screws that I couldn't tell what was bone and what was metal on the X-rays. As you can imagine, I was down pretty hard for the next eight weeks recovering from the initial crash. I became reacquainted with crutches and moved from my chair to the bathroom to the bed and back to the chair again on a regular basis. I tried to read more than watch TV. The TV was so brainless, however, I could truly relax and fall asleep whenever I watched it. I never really thought about how many organisms and bacteria live in a freshwater lake until I ripped my foot off in one and it became infected. On top of everything I had going on with my foot, it was now infected to the point where I was in need of a direct line to my heart to deliver the antibiotics needed to fight the infection. The PICC line (peripherally inserted central catheter), as it is called, delivered the drugs to my system twice a day for 30 days. The line was placed into my right arm with a tube that reached to my heart. It was quite the process of administering my daily doses of antibiotics. Cleanliness is paramount with an exact procedure taught to my wife and I by the glorious nurses who came to the house to take care of me.

I like to tell people I have a story for just about everything. It's my job; I now run a museum and I better know all the stories. Well, this story involves the PICC line running in my body. The nurses would come by once a week to change out my dressing and check on the function of the PICC line. On the same day this was scheduled, my partner Master Chief, Ken, was coming by to discuss Navy SEAL Museum business. In preparation for the nurse's visit, I administered my antibiotics as per schedule and waited for the nurse to arrive when completed. As I sat there watching TV, my friend Ken came by, walked into the living room, and immediately started yelling. "Dude, you are bleeding out!" I looked down and saw a large pool of my own blood soaking into the carpet underneath my chair. I immediately realized I had forgotten to shut off the port in my PICC line and was sitting fat, dumb, and happy bleeding out in my own living room. I turned the port off and acted like it was no big deal. A little blood never hurt anyone. I later watched my lovely bride clean up my blood in tears. Ken looked at me like I was an idiot. The nurse never heard this story when she came in to check on me. Bottom line: It never hurts to have another set of eyes to check your work, especially when it involves life and death.

After two separate rounds of PICC lines, and two years of trying to heal something that could never be healed, I decided amputation was the best course of action for me. Numerous doctors' visits convinced me I would be going through multiple surgeries for the rest of my life and the bone infection I had developed would never go away. Seemed like a "no brainer" when I made the decision. I had not been able to run or put any real pressure on my right ankle, without extreme pain, for over two years. I have known over a dozen amputees who had lost various body parts, due to combat or other reasons, leading successful lives, including actively serving on a SEAL Team. Done deal, let's chop it off. Not so fast. I did not foresee two major impacts on my decision. The first, my wife. She was not as enthused with the decision as I was. I can't blame her. This was really unknown territory we were going into. I know she would be my primary care giver while I was recovering and I had to have her total support and buy-in. The other factor was finding a doctor willing to do the procedure, believe it or not. What I didn't realize at the time was the majority of the best amputee doctors (for lack of a better term) are ER surgeons. Makes sense because they see most of the accidents which require amputations. Most other amputations are diabetes related. After seeing multiple orthopedic specialists who wanted to "fix" me with another half dozen or more surgeries, I finally had an epiphany to call a friend of mine who was a double amputee and ask his advice. He sent me to visit his prosthetist (artificial limb specialist) to get the true scoop on what I was asking for. The visit was an eye opener. I had never seen so many amputees in one place at one time.

All were helpful and answered any and all questions for both me and my wife. The prosthetist was a first-class professional with all the answers we needed. The visit not only assured my wife of the future, but it also gave us direction on the medical side. We now had a plan and had done all our research. A fresh set of professional eyes from outside my normal circle saved the day once again. SEALs tend to call on the very best experts in their field such as marksmen, divers, jumpers, and even doctors. Once we learn what they have to teach, we use that knowledge to form the path which works for us.

When it came time to move forward with the surgery, I began to share the decision with many of my and the museum's supporters about what I was doing. All were very gracious and offered their assistance in any way possible. One group of friends from the great state of New Hampshire (Live Free or Die) directed me to another highly qualified prosthetist who in turn helped guide my wife and I on the next steps and recommended I become part of a research study on amputations. It seems the basic procedure of below the knee amputations has not changed significantly since the Civil War. Who knew? A top-notch surgeon from Brigham and Women's Hospital in Boston and the research scientists at Massachusetts Institute of Technology teamed up to come up with a procedure that ties the muscles and nerves at the end of the amputation back together in a feedback loop which allows signals to travel back and forth from the stump to the brain and back again. The Ewing Procedure, named after the first patient to undergo the operation, is designed to give the patient the perception the foot is still attached, which not only reduces or eliminates phantom pain but allows them to flex their muscles. I was all about it even though one of my good friends advised I go to the doctor who had completed hundreds of these procedures versus becoming lucky patient 13, as I was to be for the Ewing. Of course, I picked the Ewing. Thirteenth patient or not, I wanted to set myself up to be in the best position possible for the future. Who knows where we will be with amputations and prosthetics 10 to 20 years from now? In addition, calculated risks are my lifestyle. I was never the SEAL that was risk averse and not willing to take a chance. I do not believe you or anyone else wants a risk-averse SEAL protecting our country. It is in our blood from the beginning, and it is not something you can turn on and off quickly. That is why SEALs tend to want to jump out of perfectly good aircraft in the first place.

The deal was made. We were to fly to Boston for the procedure and stay in Manchester, New Hampshire, for the following eight weeks while I healed up. Thank God for good friends. Through my friends and their contacts, my wife and I were able to weather this storm as comfortably as anyone could. My wife is one of the greatest women on the planet. I am lucky to have ever met her, let alone marry her. She is also one the fittest and healthiest eaters I have ever met. When we first started dating, she always reminded me the only thing I had in my refrigerator was packaged cheese slices, store-brand yogurt, Little Debbie peanut butter cookies, and Jack Daniels. Sad, but true. I was converted quickly with no mercy and no say in the matter.

I can't say I was worried about the procedure, perhaps a little anxious and relieved at the same time. I had my wife write a note to the doctor on my bad foot for a little comic relief. "If found, please return to the Navy SEAL Museum." The surgery was uneventful from my perspective—I was out cold for seven hours. The surreal thing, however, was waking up and looking down at my feet only to realize I only had one left. It took me a few weeks for my mind to remember that, which made it very important not to fall and reinjure the amputation site during that time. The surgery went well. My new limb healed ahead of schedule and I was fortunate enough to be fitted for my first new leg at the six-week mark. Prosthetists are skilled masters at their trade. The carbon-graphite leg must fit perfectly to the limb in order to eliminate pain. No small feat considering no two legs are the same.

# CHAPTER 28

# Love / Hate

After my surgery, friends set my wife, dog, and I up in a penthouse apartment in downtown Manchester, New Hampshire, to recover. Yes, penthouse. The 12,000-square-foot luxury accommodation came complete with everything you could imagine and was constructed with glass, allowing for a 360-degree view of the surrounding greater Manchester area. It was one unbelievable place to recover from amputation surgery and it was close to Boston for follow-up appointments. The penthouse itself was last decorated in the 70s or 80s and was in perfect condition. It was a real blast from the past that my wife and I are still grateful to have experienced to this day. In the first few weeks following the amputation, I did not have a prosthetic limb and was forced to use crutches to get around. My main goal was to heal and not fall down. Most mornings I would hobble to the kitchen, make myself a cup of coffee, and sit in the bar area near a window to look out at the world around me. Like a plant. I did a lot of reading and thinking and, of course, computer work. It was a scary proposition to cut my foot off but now it was done. The waiting, thinking, and talking about the procedure was over. Now was time to heal and learn to adjust. My leg looked like that of a statue with the foot broken off. Basically, normal until the point of the cut and flat on the bottom. The surgeon, who was absolutely fantastic, used the skin from my calf to wrap around to the front of my leg. It actually feels like I am rubbing my calf when I am rubbing the bottom of my nub. Weird.

One of the things that really assisted in my healing process was my service dog Jesse. Jesse is a male Border Collie and truly man's best friend. He is always happy to see me and will do just about anything he can to assist me. I speak of this because I wouldn't have had the concept of a Military Working Dog or Service Animal had it not been for my time in the Teams.

The SEAL K9 program actually started back during the Vietnam war. Dogs had limited use in the jungles, rivers, and deltas operating alongside Navy SEAL platoons. Unfortunately, after the war, the K9s were not allowed to be returned Stateside due to government policy. Of course, the SEALs brought back a few teammates, but the program was cancelled and SEAL K9 handling became a lost art. Fast forward to 9/11. A new war was in full force in Afghanistan. The request came into SEAL Team SIX headquarters for dogs to assist with explosive protection and bite work. It seems the bad guys would take off running when told to stop and the men thought it would be better to have a dog chase down the "squirter" than to shoot them. Sound logic. The only problem was we hadn't had a dog program since Vietnam. It was left to me and another Master Chief and good friend to figure out the solution. The Military Working Dog lead service in the U.S. military is the Air Force. Pre 9/11, dogs were mainly used by military police to sniff out bombs, drugs, and catch the occasional drunken soldier or sailor. Run out of Lackland Air Force base in Texas, units from around the country would go there to get training and receive trained K9s. Once we figured out the system, we started requesting augmentation from qualified dog handlers across the forces that would volunteer to deploy with a combat-hardened SEAL Team for four months or more. At the beginning, we had enough volunteers to meet the need. After a few deployments, however, word got out that deploying with the SEAL Team wasn't that great of a deal. The chances of getting shot were greatly increased with a group that went out every night in search of bad guys. With the slow down on volunteers, we had to figure out a different plan. We brought in a third Master Chief, to run the program full time, and we let him take the reins. Our U.S. Army counterparts had already started a K9 program of their own so, instead of reinventing the wheel, we used their model with modifications to start the first full-fledged program for Naval Special Warfare since Vietnam. Soon, members were making regular buying trips to the Netherlands, which at the time was the best source for Belgian Malinois and Dutch Shepherds. These two breeds, more than any other, are the choice of the SEALs. Smaller, faster, and more aggressive than your typical German Shepherd, these dogs complement every SEAL mission practical.

I have learned a lot about military K9s and their uses: how to take care of them, how to train them, and how best not to get bit. The number one receiver of dog bites from our own dogs is the actual handler. One of my early jobs at the Command was to write up a report on every dog bite and give suggestions on how to prevent them in the future. After years of writing reports almost every week, I finally figured out it was the cost of doing business. If you want a bad-ass dog, sometimes you have to put up with a little pain, especially the handlers and the role players. Muzzle or no muzzle, these dogs live to bite and will figure out a way to hurt you should they get the command. Similar to SEALs, I suppose.

I have grown to have a love/hate relationship with the dogs at this point. The Navy SEAL Museum sources its dogs from first-rate Canadian company Baden K9. Their dogs' bloodline and instructors are impeccable, but that doesn't stop the mishaps. What I have found out, however, is these breeds are actually suited for retired Special Forces individuals suffering from PTSD or other maladies. The dogs require constant supervision and care which helps the veteran take the focus off themselves and turn it to a purpose. Although not a good mix for everyone, the Navy SEAL Museum's K9 Project hand selects and trains individuals to partner with these dogs. The program is a huge success with a long waiting list of qualified applicants. The Museum's K9 Project was designed and built around helping veterans by providing service dogs for those struggling with PTSD, TBI or any number of needs. In addition, we educate the public with demonstrations of K9 skills and obedience.

CHAPTER 29

# Stand for Something
# or Die for Nothing

Each year at the museum, we honor our fallen by swimming out the ashes of Frogmen that have passed from the beaches of the original training grounds of the Naval Combat Demolition Units in Fort Pierce, Florida, directly behind the museum. Their families attend, each receiving a folded flag on bent knee, a blessing, and a military salute. The only time a SEAL kneels to the flag is when it is draped on your teammate's casket or when the chaplain hands the folded flag to the wife and children of a fallen hero.

The museum is a 501c3 not-for-profit charity which exists to preserve the history and heritage of the Navy SEALs and our predecessors, while honoring our fallen at the Navy SEAL Memorial and caring for our families through the Trident House Charities program. We regularly conduct capabilities demonstrations, showcasing SEALs doing their job, for the public. We put on a little show to give everyone a small glimpse of what it is like to be a Navy SEAL while raising money for the museum's charitable wing.

Sunday, August 2, 2020, was a Sunday like most Sundays. Rest and relaxation until my nephew called and told me about a Twitter post which showed a video from a Navy SEAL Museum fundraiser that featured our military working K9s attacking a man wearing a football jersey over his bite suit. The football jersey was that of a player known for unapologetically disrespecting our flag and the police. The video dated back to 2018 but had now taken on a different tone in the heightened atmosphere of 2020.

This individual had begun sitting and then kneeling for the National Anthem back in 2016. I was not happy about it then and neither were many Americans. Typically, privileged millionaires do not try to deliberately irritate the very people who are supporting them, but here it was on national television for everyone to see. I thought it was just a fad, someone trying to make attention for themselves. Then he actually wore socks depicting police officers as pigs while recruiting other spoiled millionaires to kneel beside him. I let it go once again, like many of those who viewed the performance. Surely this would not last. The National Football League and the owners would not allow this type of behavior. Kneeling for the flag was the football player's God-given right in this country and I respected it. That didn't mean I had to like it. My only means of countering this sign of disrespect at the time was by not watching football.

As the kneeling continued, however, I felt I had to make more of a statement. People had to know it is not alright to kneel for the flag. Maybe they weren't being taught in school? Maybe they didn't know what the flag meant to the military and all the men and women who have given their lives for this great country? How could they not know? And how could this behavior not only be allowed, but celebrated? Maybe you can understand why, after overseeing the swimming out of ashes for so many years, I am so offended when I see others disrespect the flag and our country.

I decided I wasn't going to let it happen without a fight. I personally had the idea to dress a role player in a certain football jersey, have him kneel for the National Anthem, ask him to stand and then request the K9s assist him to stand up. It was a skit meant to fire people up. Make them proud to be an American again, but it was also meant to send a clear message. Not everyone thinks it is alright to kneel for the flag.

In the three times we performed that skit to thousands of people, many got up and cheered when the football player stood. Not one person complained, feedback was positive. I knew in the back of my mind the skit could be viewed as controversial, but could it be worse than the actual kneeling in front of millions of people during a televised football game? I didn't think so at the time. We also used other football players' jerseys to get the point across. Not that many were kneeling at the time, but they were crowd favorites to be loved or hated. Nothing more, nothing less.

After a handful of iterations of the football protest, I was asked by one of our board of directors to discontinue the use of jerseys in our demonstrations because he deemed it offensive. No problem, we moved on in 2018 and focused on other likenesses to entertain our supporters.

Fast forward to August 2020. I personally communicate with others in person, on the phone or by email, in that order preferably. I do not use or intend to ever use social media. So, when my nephew informed me the video had a few thousand hits, I merely laughed and ignored his warning. By that evening, the post had a few hundred thousand hits and I started to pay attention. I know social media can be important to the retail part of our museum business and also on the communication side of things, but I had no idea just how powerful it could be.

Soon the little video was receiving millions of views. The shit was hitting the proverbial fan. People were starting to call, email, text, and tweet. There was no context to the 2018 video compared to what was going on in 2020. Rioting, looting, killing, and defunding police are the norm now and a video depicting a football player being attacked by dogs is not good. To say the least.

The only mob I had confronted in my life was in Somalia, when I had had weapons and a whole team of professionals behind me. The Twitter mob was now going after my livelihood, the museum itself, and my reputation. I had no experience in fighting this battle. There was no point in trying to explain the video. It was meant to counter a message that was now accepted across the country on every sports field and at every sporting event. Kneeling for the flag is okay. I had failed. The demonstration, which had been meant to show a different point of view, was now being used against me. The only thing I could do at this point was take the social media beating. I never considered myself a racist, but I was called that and a lot worse. The only privilege I had in my life was growing up in a loving, intact family and serving the military and this country for over 34 years. The football player had the right to express his opinion; shouldn't all of us? Apparently not.

Plans, ideas, and statements were swirling all around me—everything from resigning to apologizing or both. The only sensible thing to do would be to fall on my sword. That is what the mob was screaming for. I saw my future at the museum as bleak indeed.

Four things turned it around for me. The first was the original idea behind the skit in the first place. That never changed and it is still not alright to kneel for the flag. The second was support from my friends and family. They knew I was not a racist and were probably there at the demonstrations when literally thousands of people stood up and cheered as the "football player" was made to stand for the Anthem. Third was time. The more we waited, the less traction the story held. According to our traction report, we went from 300,000 Facebook engagements on Monday to zero on Friday. The news cycle had killed the story and moved on. Fourth was my nephew offering an alternative to the mob. Fight back. Use their methods to turn the story in our favor and gain a much wider following across the country. With the video having now received over eight million views, that was probably nearly eight million people who hadn't previously known that a Navy SEAL Museum even existed. Of that eight million views, only about 500 negative reviews were posted and, quickly, the positive reviews were far outnumbering the negative. We did not address the video. Hope is not a strategy. Hoping the problem will go away will not work. We simply stuck to our mission statement and did not deviate. Preserve the history and heritage of the Navy SEALs, honor our fallen and support our families. Bringing in trusted advisors familiar with social media and how it works was the only answer in this case so that is exactly what we did. We brought in an outside public relations firm to help guide us through the situation. Life was starting to get back to normal when the bomb dropped.

The admiral in charge of Naval Special Warfare Command (top active-duty SEAL) released an official statement pulling support of the Navy SEAL Museum in addition to stating the video was not in keeping with the Navy SEAL Ethos. I am still not sure what part of the Ethos the video was not in keeping with. Loyalty to country and team? Persevere and thrive on adversity? Placing the welfare of others before my own? Was the video in bad taste? Probably, but it was definitely not racist when it was made in 2018 and it is definitely not racist now. Was it a freedom of speech issue? Are we only allowed to speak freely if it does not offend the social media trolls? Was it because of the stand to support our police? In a time when it is acceptable to defund or even abolish police departments, who is going to say "Stop, it is not alright." We need the police more now than ever. Look how well it is working out for the citizens in Chicago, Minneapolis, Seattle, and Portland, to name a few. And what did the admiral mean by the pulling of support? The museum is a non-profit. Maybe he was talking about moral support. Regardless, his statement hurt me and the Navy SEAL Museum to the core. So much for brotherhood. There were over 100 different ways the statement could have come out that would have been much less damaging. How about something like, "The Navy SEAL Museum has raised over 2.5 million dollars in support of our SEALs and their families since 2016. We will investigate this matter thoroughly before making any premature statements." A knee-jerk reaction from a guy who had had plenty of screw-ups of his own during his time in charge of Naval Special Warfare. Laughable. But the damage was done.

Most people outside the museum organization didn't understand that Naval Special Warfare withdrawing support really didn't mean anything. It was up to me and the team to explain the intent of the video and move forward. No whining, back tracking, or apologizing at this point. Coming out with a statement like "We are not racist" wouldn't have helped anything or anyone. The decision was made to ride it out. Take care of our supporters and donors; they understand what it is all about. By day three, the heat almost totally subsided and the texts, emails, tweets, and calls of support started flowing in at a much higher rate than the hate had. Things had just done a 180-degree turn. Donations were up, store sales were up, and we had not made any errors to make the situation worse. Everything went away and life went on.

My last thought on this story comes from another of my board of directors. He said, and many have said before him, that the museum should be apolitical or have no stance. For the most part I agree, but when cancel culture comes calling to tear down our statues representing the Vietnam and Korean wars, where will we stand then? It is easy to see a time in the future when these two wars are erased from our memories the way it is happening to the Civil War today.

# CHAPTER 30

# Never Be Afraid to Try Something New

Never quit. As former executive director and now chief executive officer of the Navy SEAL Museum, I was thrust from a military world into a business one very quickly. The military, and rightfully so, is not so worried about making money but prefers to spend it. New equipment and training are what keeps us alive and one step ahead of our enemies. The saying in the office when things go bad is "Is anyone dying?" which happens to be a legitimate question in the Special Operations world. The point is, slow down, talk the problem through, and move forward. No one's life is depending on the speed of every decision. Of course, there are always exceptions. I have done a fairly good job controlling my time online. I follow a strict schedule and try to stick to it: typical wake up between 0530 and 0600; make coffee and check email for anything of consequence that happened overnight; pay some bills as needed and then walk the dog.

There is nothing better than going for a walk first thing in the morning to clear your head. After the dog walk, it is workout time. One thing I have learned throughout my time in the Teams is that working out and staying in shape is critical to your overall mental and physical health. Besides, no one wants to listen to a fat SEAL. It is easy to stay on the workout schedule since I have been working out my entire life. Most of the time it was mandatory to stay alive. Now it is for fun on my terms and my schedule. Typical workouts revolve around swimming, running, or lifting weights. I have never been a team-sports person or had the need to work out with others. My timeline has always been tight, so I don't have time to wait for others. Additionally, are you really working out if you have the breath to talk?

On my short drive to the office, I try to listen to the news to find out what is going on in the world, which is getting harder and harder to do each day. I'm hoping for an actual news outlet that reports the news rather than focusing on the talking head that happens to be reading it. So far, no luck from either side. I don't "do" social media and never will but, believe it or not, I started a podcast. Never too old to try new things. It is called the "Friendly Fire Podcast" which covers everyday issues across the country from both a left and right point of view. With the help of a good friend and retired Marine, we spar about different subjects but remain friends, something this country should be able to do but currently does not. I am truly bewildered at times with the logic of the left, but my co-podcaster does a very good job explaining his point of view. We typically agree 50 percent of the time but totally disagree the other 50 percent. The podcast is a lot of fun to create each week and it forces me to stay up to date with the news and what is happening in the world. Never be afraid to try something new.

# CHAPTER 31

# Doing the Right Thing Regardless of How It Looks

The Navy SEAL Museum has a scholarship program run through the Trident House Charities Program. It is a great way for future college kids of Special Operations warriors to get a leg up on tuition costs, which seem to be astronomical. The scholarships also cover younger children attending private school since many of the places SEALs are assigned around the world may not have the best education system. One such scholarship is sponsored by a major applicant to the museum who I know very well. I would have to say a majority of the people I deal with on a day-to-day basis would call themselves "conservative," which is a dirty word in some parts of the country. This applicant is a self-made success and has donated over five hundred thousand dollars to the scholarship fund to help the children of both Army and Naval Special Forces. It came as a surprise to me recently to receive an email from one of the museum's advisory board of directors stating the applicant was not happy with some of the questions being asked as part of the scholarship application. To tell you the truth, I had not read the application, or the questions, which was a mistake. Not that I would have changed anything, but I wouldn't have been caught off guard when the email came in.

The complaint was that the questions were biased and should be removed from the application or that the museum should separate any relationship with the applicant if the questions did not change. Classic cancel culture. First thing I did was write back that I would look into it.

Second thing I did was bring up the application online to read the questions. Here is one:

> Currently "Big Tech" is censoring free speech in our country. Given that these are unelected organizations, individuals and their influencers, it is completely inconsistent with our First Amendment and is potentially very dangerous. What, in your opinion, needs to be done to correct this violation of our rights?

Is it a bit leading? Yes, but any high school graduate should be able to answer this question no matter their political leanings. The cancel culture was coming after us once again and we had to figure out the best way to handle the situation without backing down. The solution ended up being quite simple. There was no pulling back the questions even if we wanted to. The application had been posted for a few weeks and there was no way to track how many kids had downloaded the paperwork and had begun to fill it out. We decided to pull the application offline and provide it to anyone that called and asked for it. Win-win. The application was no longer online, but still available to the kid who needs a scholarship and recognizes the questions for what they are: a means to an end to help pay for college.

A past leader of the Navy SEALs was recently interviewed and asked what was the greatest asset of Naval Special Warfare today? His reply? Diversity and inclusivity. Yes, that is what he said. Sure, he said more after that, but I do not have the stomach to repeat it. And here all these years I thought our ability to complete our mission no matter the circumstance was our greatest asset. I thought having men and women ready, willing, and able to fight to defend our country was our greatest asset. The U.S. Navy has spent a lot of time and energy trying to figure out how to recruit minorities for SEAL training but also how to recruit the non-minority applicant. There is no black, white, or brown in the SEAL Teams. You either do your job or you don't. Reputation is everything.

# Epilogue

I recently had one of the greatest honors I have ever had along with one of the saddest times of my life. All in one day. I planned and led the Swim Out for my first mentor Rudy Boesch.

Each set of ashes is carried to sea by two SEALs, active or retired, from the beaches directly behind the museum. Friends and family gather along with regular people who have no tie to the heroes we are swimming out other than wanting to pay their respects.

The same beaches Rudy had trained on in World War II were now going to be his final resting ground. Our chaplain, my friend, took care of each of the 15 families on the beach that day like they were his own. Each received a folded flag on bent knee, a blessing, and a military salute.

I gave the order for the SEALs to march to the sea and off the 30 Frogmen swam with their precious cargo. Once at a safe distance at sea, they released their brothers and returned to the beach to greet and console the families. Rudy had made it full circle.

As everyone departed, I brought up the rear. We walked by the Navy SEAL Memorial with the current 309 names of the Frogmen who have died in combat or in training since World War II.

With approximately 17,000 Frogmen produced in eighty years, your odds of knowing a SEAL, let alone meeting one, are fairly slim. Eight thousand were produced in World War II, with only 100–150 graduating BUD/S training each year since. With our numbers so small, at only 2,500 active-duty SEALs at any given time, the loss of only one SEAL is devastating to the force. Now imagine a helicopter full.

If you are lucky enough to visit the Museum, take a minute and walk out on the beach, bow your head, and thank God for creating men like Rudy Boesch who were willing to give everything for us.

Rudolph Ernst Boesch
1928–2019

Master Chief Rudy Boesch on fast rope acquired from British Special Forces, circa 1976.